P3ø

P9-CLH-618

The Making of the 20th Century

This series of specially commissioned titles focuses attention on significant and often controversial events and themes of world history in the present century. Each book provides sufficient narrative and explanation for the newcomer to the subject while offering, for more advanced study, detailed source-references and bibliographies, together with interpretation and reassessment in the light of recent scholarship.

In the choice of subjects there is a balance between breadth in some spheres and detail in others; between the essentially political and matters economic or social. The series cannot be a comprehensive account of everything that has happened in the twentieth century, but it provides a guide to recent research and explains something of the times of extraordinary change and complexity in which we live. It is directed in the main to students of contemporary history and international relations, but includes titles which are of direct relevance to courses in economics, sociology, politics and geography.

The Making of the 20th Century

Series Editor: GEOFFREY WARNER

Titles in the Series include

Already published

Titles in preparation include

Race, Conflict and the International Order

From Empire to United Nations

Hugh Tinker

ST. JOSEPH'S UNIVERSITY   STX
HT1521.T56 1977b
Race, conflict, and the international or

3 9353 00077 7316

HT
1521
.T56
1977b

179686

© Hugh Tinker 1977

All rights reserved. No part of this publication
may be reproduced or transmitted, in any form
or by any means, without permission.

First edition 1977
Reprinted 1979
Published by
THE MACMILLAN PRESS LTD
London and Basingstoke
Associated companies in Delhi Dublin
Hong Kong Johannesburg Lagos Melbourne
New York Singapore and Tokyo

ISBN 0 333 19664 3 (hard cover)
0 333 19665 1 (paper cover)

Printed in Great Britain by
REDWOOD BURN LIMITED
Trowbridge & Esher

This book is sold subject to the standard
conditions of the Net Book Agreement

The paperback edition of this book is sold subject to the condition
that it shall not, by way of trade or otherwise, be lent, resold, hired
out, or otherwise circulated without the publisher's prior consent,
in any form of binding or cover other than that in which it is
published and without a similar condition including this condition
being imposed on the subsequent purchaser.

Contents

The illustration on the front of the cover is reproduced by permission of the Associated Press, London.

For
my grandson

Joshua

May he find
the twenty-first century more kind

Preface

The factor of race enters increasingly into our lives at every level. It has been approached in the past on a personal, social level ('Would you like your daughter to marry a black man?') but in the 1970s it has attained the importance of a world phenomenon. This book was first planned in December 1974, and writing was begun in December 1975. Even during the brief intervening period, the importance of race in world affairs has dramatically increased. Probably, before this book is published a further escalation will have occurred. Yet, thus far, few writers have attempted to explore the international dimensions of race. Ronald Segal's *The Race War* seemed sensational when it appeared in 1966; it suffered from the author's tendency to introduce events and trends which were outside the orbit of race and thereby it had the effect of seeming to strain too hard to make a case.

Several shorter studies have examined the subject. Perhaps the most incisive and articulated is by A. R. Preiswerk, 'Race and Colour in International Relations' in *The Year Book of World Affairs, 1970* (London, 1970). More free-ranging but also stimulating is Harold R. Isaacs's 'Color in World Affairs', *Foreign Affairs* (New York, January 1969), while a more basic approach is taken by Robert K. A. Gardiner, 'Race and Color in International Relations,' in *Color and Race*, edited by John Hope Franklin (Boston, 1968). The present study has drawn upon these articles, especially that of A. R. Preiswerk, but is based more upon the author's own observations and experiences. (A valuable stimulus was given by an unpublished paper of J. D. B. Miller, 'Racial Equality', delivered at the Institute of Commonwealth Studies, University of London, in October 1956, at a time when most of us had no idea that race would become a prime factor in international relations.)

The work was supported by a Fellowship from the Rockefeller Foundation in the programme on conflict in international relations.

At the outset, we need to find some answer to that elusive question: What is Race? In the United States, a person with a skin of a light colour with even one remote black ancestor is black; whereas in Brazil a person with a skin of a dark colour with even one remote white ancestor is not black. Race lies in the eye of the beholder. We shall not now try to provide a comprehensive definition of race which can withstand all biological, cultural, religious and political criteria. The reader is asked to accept the following working definitions. We have a *racial* factor when one group of people, united by their own perception of inherited and distinctive qualities, are set apart from another group with (supposedly) separate inherited and distinctive qualities. We have a *racist* factor when one group claims a dominant position, justified by the supposed inferiority of the other group. This superiority will be claimed on the basis of physical characteristics, but is reinforced by a claim to spiritual and mental superiority, or what Arnold Toynbee calls 'psychic qualities'. It may be hoped that before the reader has finished with this book he or she will have formulated a more satisfactory definition.

November 1976   HUGH TINKER

1 Race and the Contemporary World

DURING the nineteenth century power and wealth became concentrated in that section of the world which is predominantly white; this book deals with the consequences of that concentration in which black and brown became subject to white. In the nineteenth century this polarisation was (relatively) unchallenged and unchallengeable. In the early twentieth century it was questioned, but many were still prepared to defend white supremacy. In mid-century the challenge was more powerfully pressed by a new combination of forces: the nations of the Third World, revolutionary communism, and the depressed non-white minorities of the wealthy white countries. Just as the white countries do not represent a monolithic bloc, but are mutually competitive, so the challengers are more disunited than united. Nevertheless, there is an opposing alignment of peoples, powers and principles.

This book is an attempt to study in a global context how white bastions have cracked, though not fallen. Most studies of race concentrate upon one country, or within that country focus upon a city or a neighbourhood. In that more limited context, the issues and the people concerned can be sharply differentiated. In Atlanta, Georgia, or in South Africa, the composition of the powerholders, the composition of the challengers, the strategies of repression and resistance are clearly revealed. Within the world context the boundaries become blurred. Do we align the Soviet Union with the white bloc, or with the Third World challenge, or must we exclude the U.S.S.R. from the analysis? How far is the struggle between multinational industrial giants and organised labour a colourblind struggle in which class and the profit motive are the only key variables?

We are concerned to trace the dissolution – partial rather than complete – of white dominance. It involves the almost complete breakdown of a system of 'superiority' beliefs and values at the level of rational, conscious assertion and also the partial breakdown – at any rate the transformation – of the international structure of power; all within the twentieth century, and to a great extent since the Second World War.

The polarisation of power and wealth around north-western Europe and the United States in the nineteenth century was based first upon the development of an advanced system of banking, credit and insurance – the money market – and also upon advances in the system of trade and communication. Relatively small countries, especially England and the Netherlands, accumulated a great surplus of wealth. Despite England's lead in the industrial revolution, power gradually shifted and industrial productivity, based upon large units and rapid adaptation to technological change, led to the emergence of Germany and the United States as the economic giants. The growth of Western commercial and industrial wealth depended partly upon the penetration of the rest of the world, both to provide raw materials and to provide a mass market for the mass production of Western industry: 'Oil for the Lamps of China', and profits for Standard Oil of New Jersey.

This polarisation of power within the group of nations variously described as Anglo-Saxon, Teutonic, or Nordic was accompanied by an unprecedented traffic with other peoples. The encounter seemed to confirm the West in its sense of superiority: as early as 1835, G. M. Macaulay observed that 'A single shelf of a good European library was worth the whole native literature of India and Arabia.'[1] Yet there were hostile anti-white reactions, such as the Great Revolt in India in 1857 and the Boxer Rising in China in 1899. The Anglo-Saxons (whom we may label the Anglo) grew ever more conscious of their superiority; they were also uneasily aware of their vulnerability. The two great theories which were invoked to explain race in the nineteenth century hinged upon these two opposites.

Joseph-Arthur de Gobineau (1816–82) was a French civil servant, diplomat and novelist of aristocratic origin. To him, the French Revolution was a cataclysmic mistake; men were born, and remained, *unequal*. His *Essai sur l'inégalité des races humaines*, published in four volumes, 1853–5, was a refutation of the Revolution. Certain of the revolutionary publicists (according to Arnold Toynbee)[2] had proclaimed that the French nobility were descended from the Frankish conquerors of the Gauls, and after fourteen centuries revenge was exacted when they were banished once again into the Rhineland.*

---

* Toynbee in his *Study of History* refutes the theory that civilisations are linked with inherently superior racial types. However, in his survey of world civilisations (really empires) he finds that the European races have founded more civilisations than anyone, and he concludes: 'The Black races alone have not contributed positively to any civilisation – yet.' (Abridged version, p. 54.) Is there an unconscious racial assumption here? There is in most of us.

Gobineau took up this myth and announced that the Franks – whom he identified with the ancient Aryans, emerging from primeval Prussia – were indeed the aristocrats, a 'race of masters' who had breathed life into the Roman Empire. Their decline had been due to mixing their race with other inferior races. Such a mixing was an inevitable feature of democracy, the force which he conceived was destroying his motherland, France.

These ideas were most eagerly absorbed in Germany, where a Gobineau club was founded with Wagner as its most celebrated member. His operas were redolent of legendary Nordic heroism and Aryan glory. One of Wagner's daughters married Houston Stewart Chamberlain (1855–1926), the nephew of two Indian Army generals, who became a naturalised German. His book, *The Foundations of the Nineteenth Century* (1899), emphasised the essential need to enshrine the race within the nation-state. He observed: 'Wherever, as in India, nations are not formed, the stock of strength that has been gathered by race decays. . . . The firm national union . . . fixes the existing bond of blood and impels us to make it ever closer.' This was the seed-bed from which came Hitler's belief in *Blut und Boden*, 'Blood and Soil', and led to the cry *Ein Volk, Ein Reich, Ein Führer*.

Gobinism, as it was called, had little influence outside Germany, and in Britain and America the belief in racial superiority owed most to the publication in 1859 of Charles Darwin's *The Origin of Species*. Darwin (1809–82) did not himself apply his theory of natural selection from the animal world to human-kind. Nor did he coin the phrase 'the survival of the fittest' (though he accepted it as a chapter heading from Herbert Spencer). But by analogy from the animal world, his exponents sought to demonstrate that the emergence of the Anglo as the dominant race was scientifically inevitable. Darwin described how all animal life was in competition for scarce resources. The successful animals were those who adapted themselves over untold generations to compete, in order to obtain their food and to defend themselves against rivals and the natural environment. The unsuccessful animals gradually failed to hold on to the necessary resources, and dwindled in number until they became extinct. It was possible for primitive types to survive only when they were so isolated as to have no competitors. (But Darwin was not really seeking to prove that all life was a progression to the highest. He insisted: 'The survival of the fittest does not necessarily include progressive development. . . . And it may be asked what advantage . . . would it be . . . to an earthworm to be highly organized.')

For those seeking a scientific justification for Anglo dominance there was plenty they could cite from Darwin. He produced evidence to show that 'hybridism' is most frequently sterile: justification for preserving the 'purity' of the race. He declared, 'I am inclined to believe that largeness of area is still more important, especially for the production of species which shall prove capable of enduring for a long period and of spreading widely': justification for empire. Out of all this emerged the conviction that the white race was thousands of years ahead of the other races.[3] The Anglo-Americans began to believe they had a 'manifest destiny' to inherit the earth, because the white race had demonstrated supreme adaptability and capability. The phenomenon of Anglo emigration and colonisation showed that they were now equipped to take over the world. In the face of their challenge, inferior races would dwindle and become extinct: it was inevitable. The fate of the Australian bushman and the North American Indian was a proof of their inability to compete, and their fate was certain to overtake other backward races. The blacks in America and the Caribbean, though freed from slavery, must certainly join the American Indian in final oblivion. In South Africa it was inevitable that the Hottentots and Kaffirs would perish and the land be taken over by British and Afrikaners: provided the latter could successfully adapt to the challenge of the superior British.

Something of this racial pyramid of power is perceived in the analysis produced by Jawaharlal Nehru when in a British-Indian prison:

The British are an insular race, and long success and prosperity has made them look down on almost all others. For them, as some one has said, '*Les nègres commencent à Calais*'. But that is too general a statement. Perhaps the British upper-class division of the world would be somewhat as follows: (1) Britain – a long gap, and then (2) The British Dominions (white population only) and America (Anglo-Saxon only, and not dagoes, wops, etc.), (3) Western Europe, (4) Rest of Europe (5) South America (Latin races), a long gap, and then (6) the brown, yellow and black races of Asia and Africa, all hunched up more or less together. How far we of the last of these classes are from the heights where our rulers live![4]

This biting commentary was all too near the standard Anglo view of the world.

This conception of the triumph of the Anglo was an important feature of political doctrine and political programmes as the twentieth century dawned. In Britain, the imperialist Joseph Chamberlain advocated an alliance of Great Britain, the United States and Germany. In America, Theodore Roosevelt, while excluding the un-American concept of alliances from his philosophy, certainly envisaged two great empires sharing the world, with the United States dominating the Americas and the Pacific, and Britain supreme in South Asia and Africa. Even Kaiser Wilhelm II, after the Boxer Rising in China, conceived of an Anglo-Teutonic mission to wipe out the Yellow Peril.

These beliefs entered the realm of popular literature, and again attained a kind of trans-national, Anglo acceptance. Rudyard Kipling (1865–1936), the British imperialist who saw Africans and Asians as the 'lesser breeds without the law', adjured his readers to 'take up the white man's burden'. He was actually urging the Americans in the Philippines to join hands with the British in India. Jack London (1876–1916), the American socialist, alerted his readers to the Yellow Peril and preached the superiority of the white race: his books were as acceptable in Britain as in his own land. (The three best-selling English-language novelists in the Soviet Union are, in descending order, Kipling, London, Dickens. This says something about the extent to which unconscious racial superiority transcends political cultures.)

A world in which Anglo domination formed the natural international order was given institutional shape by the recognition of new forms of political hegemony. Before the nineteenth century the colony was an extension of the mother country (like the American or Australian colonies). From about 1870 a new form of colonialism became paramount in which Western states annexed vast areas of Africa and Asia, which could never become 'white man's country'. The political and philosophical justification was that the 'advanced' white powers would act as tutors or trustees for their Asian or African wards who, in the fullness of time (and this was conceived in terms of hundreds of years), would be capable of behaving in a civilised manner.

It was beyond the capacity of Britain, Germany, the United States or France to absorb the whole non-white world into their colonies, but other devices were available. The blessing of tutelage might be partially bestowed by making an African or Asian country a 'protectorate'; that is, by permitting the indigenous system of rulership and administration to function under the 'indirect rule' of a white supervisor, designated the Resident or the Agent. An even more vague form of tutelage was evolved – that of the 'zone of influence', whereby a Western power gave notice to its rivals that it had assumed a vague responsibility for looking after the region.

Where the rival imperial powers were not prepared to concede the dominant role to another they devised ways of sharing out the task of tutelage. Thailand provided an extreme example, with a British adviser in charge of finance, an American adviser to reform the legal system, German advisers developing railways, and Danish advisers training the police and armed services. Similarly, in China – although Britain had established pre-eminence (and a British official was at the head of the customs department, providing the bulk of the revenue) – there was broad Western participation in the development of railways and other profitable enterprises.

Western superiority was explicitly demonstrated in the legal concept of extra-territoriality, applied in countries where international rivalry excluded the introduction of direct or indirect colonial rule. Within the Ottoman Empire, China, Thailand, and many other states which were formally sovereign, the white nations claimed that their people could not be made subject to the legal system because it could not pass what might be termed 'the civilisation test'. These states were therefore compelled to admit the establishment of special courts which might be mixed, with local and foreign judges sitting together, or more often foreign, consular courts in which the local legal system had no authority. In any dispute between a national of the country and a foreigner from the West, the case would be taken to the 'civilised' court.

Extra-territoriality was an example of how the Western powers successfully created an inter-national system responsive to themselves alone. By the beginning of the twentieth century there was a generally accepted inter-national system, bringing together the 'civilised' nations under recognised rules, boundaries, limitations. Vessels trading across the oceans were legally under 'international law'. Even in time of war, a set of rules was generally recognised: the Geneva Convention, developed from 1864 onward.

During the nineteenth century, people within states – individuals and groups – were brought more and more within the ambit of the state. The international system provided a superior level or stratum of control. States were increasingly brought into a 'contractual' relationship with each other by treaties and agreements, just as individuals or firms were within a contractual relationship in their own countries.

This book is concerned with the erosion of white hegemony; substantially in the area of belief, and partially in the area of institutionalised control.

To a considerable extent, the Western empires brought about their own downfall by their mutual jealousies and ambitions. Their carefully devised regulations could not provide an organisation capable of satisfying them all, not all the time. Hence, they eventually resorted to internecine war. The Western empires were also challenged by a new, non-Western empire: that of Japan. Japan's steady rise to great power status involved the near-collapse of Imperial Russia, an assertion of Japanese primacy among the competitors for control over China, and – briefly but with enormous consequences – the overthrow of the empires of Britain, France, the Netherlands and the United States in South-east Asia.[5]

The assault on the empires also came from the revolutionary movements generated by and emerging from the Soviet Union, Communist China, and Communist Vietnam. This, above all, gave the struggle against white dominance an ideological and motivational drive. Even where the 'freedom movements' were not organised on communist or even Marxist lines they derived borrowed strength from the idea of revolution. Probably no other word was so often invoked – the Indonesian revolution, the Burmese revolution, the Ghanaian or Zairean revolution: all had in common the belief that white colonialism could be overturned.

Cause and effect became intertwined: it is frequently asserted that the collapse of Western imperialism was caused by a loss of nerve. The proclaiming of liberal principles, and enthusiasm for equality and the rights of man, so much on the lips of British statesmen as they participated in the 'transfer of power' – especially in the 1940s and 1950s, before the whole process became routine – was not much more than a cover for their inner acknowledgement of weakness. The loss of nerve spread – to the Dutch, to the French, and at last to the Americans in Vietnam. Only in South Africa it will be said, there are white men who have not lost their nerve because they still live under the shadow of Cecil Rhodes and 'Oom Paul' Kruger.

Besides the collapse of the imperialist idea there was a massive shaking up of the international system. The First World War destroyed for ever a system based upon alliances and the 'balance of power'. It brought into the states-system new countries established on the principle of 'national self-determination', inherently unstable and vulnerable. It threw up a 'rogue elephant', the Soviet Union, which had no recognised place in the international system. The First World War left the Western empires apparently intact – apart from that of

Germany, whose colonial wealth was redistributed to inflate the British and French empires to their largest limits. The world had to wait for the Second World War and its aftermath to witness the almost total dissolution of the old system. Again, a great rogue elephant emerged – Communist China. Whereas after 1918 the Western powers adjusted to the Soviet Union (and vice versa) within ten years, China remained – or was kept – out of the Western system for almost thirty years.

The exclusion of China weakened the legitimacy of the established international system, but perhaps even more deleterious was the dissolving of many of the supports which had previously distinguished the inter-national from the internal politics of the world. New forms of activity emerged – the most far-reaching being the guerrilla resistance movement – which challenged the whole conception of international order. In some instances the guerrillas attained national and in-ternational status; as did the Viet Minh and Viet Cong. In other instances they slowly faded out of view, as did Biafra. But others persist – very much in evidence, yet impossible to organise into the system – the most pressing and urgent being the Palestine Liberation Organisation.

Efforts have been made to oppose these elusive, 'neither local nor national' forces by other organisations which are also elusive. Dominat-ing all is the American Central Intelligence Agency (C.I.A.) which can only be called extra-national or ultra-state. Other, frightening, mani-festations of these counter-revolutionary activities emergrd in the Congo and in Angola. The domain of international relations has lost its clarity.

While the Western white empires have all been formally dissolved (apart from vestigial fragments like Hong Kong or Puerto Rico) the phenomenon of neo-colonialism persists. Driven into their inner bastions, the former imperial powers have succeeded in mounting a second industrial revolution based upon high technology, which leaves the rest of the world dependent upon their computers, their electronics, their supersonic aircraft, their missiles and space stations. Western industry has lifted up the white workforce into a status that is virtually middle class: in Marxist terms, the workers have been co-opted by the bourgeoisie. There has been a pulling apart of the classes, with the superior workers co-opted into the middle class, and the roles they formerly discharged being taken by a proletariat – or sub-proletariat – recruited from the former colonial Third World countries.

When the non-whites were controlled by their imperial masters within their own distant countries, the gap between rulers and ruled permitted a blurring of racial or racist assertions of superiority. The imperial system was in control, and any black or brown subjects who arrived in the *métropole* as students, or even as permanent residents, formed no threat and could be easily accepted. In the imperial aftermath, with a large black and brown workforce actually within the metropolitan country, there was a tangible threat. In a sense, the anti-colonial freedom movements had now arrived within the imperial, or ex-imperial gates. The challenges which brought about the collapse of white supremacist ideology and the erosion of the international power system threaten the continuation of prevailing structures of power internally. At a time when the West has to accommodate Third World demands at the international level, it is increasingly resisting demands made internally, within the metropolitan redoubt.

The relationship between whites and non-whites has been greatly modified by becoming a worldwide relationship. When white dominance was at its peak it was usual for relations between governors and governed to be regulated by many different sets of rules to meet local requirements. Where non-whites were an insignificant minority, as in Europe or the northern United States, it was unnecessary to lay down rules; and it was usual to argue that these were open societies, accepting all without reference to skin-colour. Where whites were a small (though dominant) minority, as in India or tropical Africa, their power rested upon the support of administrators, police, soldiers, largely drawn from the subject people. Often a 'Divide and Rule' policy was developed, exploiting pre-existing differences between the indigenous communities; but over all, it was unnecessary to devise rules to separate whites and non-whites.

Where whites formed a settler or 'boss' class within a mainly black or brown population, as in South Africa or Kenya, it was considered vitally necessary to enforce a complete set of rules to ensure white supremacy in every way: political, social, economic. In the American South, blacks formed an actual majority in one state only – Mississippi – though throughout the South they formed between one-third and one-quarter of the total population. This situation appeared even more threatening to white supremacy than in a 'settler' context: for it was in the American South that the rules, and their enforcement, were most rigorous.

Until Gunnar Myrdal wrote of an *American Dilemma*, most northern

Americans thought that the South had its own problem, arising out of its 'peculiar institution', slavery. During the 1950s, the United States discovered that the problem was nationwide: and went on to realise that it is worldwide.

For the transforming change is that white racism can no longer shelter in its own particular environment. It has to face world exposure. The change has partly arisen as empires and the imperial idea became unfashionable. It has partly come about as the result of black and brown protest and revolt. In this book the transformation in the position of South Africa will be examined as a particularly striking example of how the attitudes and policies of other white powers have swung right round.

It must be emphasised that it is white racism which is transfixed under the world searchlight. Other forms of racism are seen as less obnoxious: as perhaps they are. Black and brown opinion holds that any attempt to focus on phenomena such as Amin in Uganda is merely an attempt to shift the spotlight away from white racism.

*

The present work involves two fields of study: those of race relations and international relations. Both are strangely similar; unkind pedagogic persons might describe them as 'non-subjects'. Both call upon, and stray into, a number of disciplines: contemporary history, politics, economics, law, sociology – and, for race relations, anthropology. Both are recent fields of study, emerging in pioneer form in the 1920s and 1930s, and gaining full acceptance (if, indeed, they are yet altogether accepted) in the 1960s and 1970s. Both emerged as 'action' subjects; those who took them up believed that serious study could have repercussions upon actual circumstances. Both developed in response to a growing sense of crisis: a feeling that things were getting out of control.

Other disciplines have come into being in response to an urge to put things right. Almost every serious philosopher, from Plato to Locke and Rousseau and on to Mill and Marx, has evolved his philosophy in order to create a better world, as he sees it. All the social sciences – politics, economics, sociology, etc. – have an action, or 'policy' aspect.* In-

---

* Gunnar Myrdal observes: 'There can be no such thing as disinterested research. Valuations enter into social research not only when drawing policy conclusions but already when searching for facts and when establishing the relationship between facts. To have a view of society assumes a viewpoint' – Myrdal, 'Biases in Social Research', in Arne Tiselius and Sam Nilsson (eds), *The Place of Value in a World of Facts* (Stockholm, 1970) pp. 160–1.

ternational relations and race relations studies only seem different
because they were demonstrably evolved very recently in response to
actual needs and demands within the present generation.

Another questionable characteristic of the two fields is their concern
with prediction. Serious scholars are constantly required to project their
studies so as to demonstrate what consequences will follow from the
escalation of certain situations or the adoption of certain policies.
Again, this is not peculiar to these fields: we are all familiar with the
downward or upward turning curves of the economist, leading to
scarcity or plenty. Yet somehow it does often seem that neither race
relations nor international relations has acquired a sufficiently
'scientific' technique to make prediction much more than assertion,
often based upon implicit or explicit political assumptions.

For another common feature of the two fields is that they cannot
function in a 'pure' or 'objective' environment. Their practitioners have
different models of society and the political order which determine their
different approaches. Broadly speaking, we can distinguish three
approaches: the liberal, the conservative, and the revolutionary.

The social sciences in Britain and the United States are predominantly liberal in outlook: so much so, that the liberal is the only one
who is not given a label. It is assumed that the liberal is the truly
objective, truly detached academic analyst. The liberal is an heir to the
Darwinian philosophy; he believes that a process of evolution is at work,
whereby lower forms give way to higher forms. He does not deal in
hundreds of thousands of years, but in decades: yet he still does insist on
a time-scale for change: 'It will work, given time . . . given time' is his
favourite advice. Liberalism has discarded nineteenth century *laissez-
faire* in favour of twentieth-century *étatisme*; change must be given a
discreet push by state action; the contemporary liberal is an institution
man. But he still believes firmly that society and the political order must
take as the starting-point things as they are.

In international relations, liberal scholars have been assiduous in
promoting international institutions to resolve conflict and bring about
greater world harmony. Most still cherish some latter-day Benthamite
notion of consensus, 'the greatest happiness of the greatest number'; the
aggregation of pleasure; the minimisation of pain. They believe in
international law, international co-operation and aid in development;
the amelioration of causes of tension. In short, they still believe in
evolution, or what the men of the nineteenth century called progress.

Liberal thought also dominates the field of race relations. There is enormous emphasis upon the promotion of beneficent institutions; machinery to overcome discrimination, to tackle the worst manifestations of urban poverty, equal opportunity programmes, and above all, education . . . education. Liberal race relations policies are almost all designed to level up comparable blacks to comparable whites; there is no desire to overhaul the entire structure of society. The goal is always harmony, and the underlying assumption is that a kind of 'natural harmony' exists which is threatened by white racial discrimination and by a black backlash. Despite all our experience, we are still investing heavily in progress.

In the late 1960s and 1970s, international relations studies began to move in the direction of conservatism; though those involved called themselves 'realists' (the liberals are called 'idealists'). Their approach is to accept conflict as the natural condition of the inter-national scene and to study how a country (invariably their country) can best meet the various forms of conflict to which it may be exposed. Strategic studies became important, leading to 'futurism' and the Herman Kahn school of doomwatchers. Others launched into 'games theory' – the tactics and strategy of international challenge and response, and evolved theories of crisis management. The idea behind most of these studies is the principle which motivated Confucius, namely that there is a grave danger of everything getting much worse, and that the best formula is to hold on to what exists at present: the devil we know.

Race relations has not really produced any significant conservative scholars; though some are inclined that way. There are those who predicate a 'wave' theory of race relations, arguing that the periods of crisis – as in the late 1960s in the United States – will be followed by periods of relaxed tension. There are even some scholars who advocate *laissez-faire* strategies, the most notable being Daniel P. Moynihan with his policy of 'benign neglect'.

Race relations studies have diverged from the predominantly liberal pattern (especially in Britain, and to a lesser extent in north-west Europe) in producing a serious quantity of revolutionary literature. Most of this school are Marxists – though by no means all Marxist scholars are revolutionaries.[6] These studies almost invariably begin with an analysis of capitalist institutions, which are seen as a carefully devised structure of repression, with the police having a key role as agents of repression. The black population – which term invariably includes all non-whites – are the main target for planned repression, because as a sub-proletariat, an under-class, they are the natural agents of revolution. The white workers are assumed to have been co-opted by capitalism by 'token' concessions which cause them to identify with the middle class.

There is a definite cleavage between those who envisage the black proletariat as the vanguard of a working class mobilised into full consciousness of class solidarity and militancy, and others who classify the white workers among the enemies of the black proletariat and who therefore envisage a revolution which involves the total destruction of white society and its replacement by a new order emerging out of the Third World. As Stokely Carmichael declared at Havana in 1967: 'The American working class enjoys the fruits of the labour of the Third World Workers. The proletariat has become the Third World; the bourgeoisie is White Western society.'[7]

International relations has responded less obviously to the new wave of revolutionary thinking. There is the conception of 'under-development' as a deliberate policy of Western international cap-italism, designed to strip Africa, Asia and Latin America and reduce them to poverty in the interests of the West. There is also the furore in America following the publication of the Pentagon Papers and the disastrous conclusion to the American Twenty Years War in Vietnam. These two impulses may soon have a major impact on international relations studies. Already there is a massive revision of the conventional conception of the American role as upholder of liberty, and a more rigorous analysis of American aggression, for example, in the light of C.I.A. support for fascism in Chile.

*

The present study is conceived upon 'revolutionary' lines, though the author would be classified as the mildest of liberals. The period surveyed begins with the climacteric moment of popular white imperialism, around the time of Queen Victoria's Diamond Jubilee, and ends with the moving of the resolution condemning Zionism 'as a form of racism' in the United Nations General Assembly in November 1975, and the growing momentum towards racial conflict in Africa in 1976.

Within this period, it is argued that the actual nature of the 'relations' between white rulers and black and brown subjects, and between whites and blacks in any given society, is one of conflict, and that the working out of the dialectic of conflict was 'revolutionary' in the sense that a world order and world belief-system has been overthrown. In the aftermath of empire, that conflict has slackened in certain directions and intensified in others. Prediction is avoided in this study, but it may well prove that the U.N. resolution linking Israel and racism introduced a new era in international race encounters.

2 Imperial High Noon

'WHAT is Empire but the predominance of Race?', exclaimed Lord Rosebery the Liberal Imperialist in 1900 at the height of the war in South Africa: 'How marvellous it all is! . . . Do we not hail, in this, less the energy and fortune of a race than the supreme direction of the Almighty?'[1] Whether God or the white mystique was the prime cause, the expansion of Europe led to several different kinds of empire; all involved the reinforcement of white dominance. White immigrants sometimes entered lands declared to be virgin, empty, free for settlement, but these lands were the homes of hunters and pastoralists: the Bushmen of Australia, or the Indians of the American prairie. Other temperate lands where whites arrived to settle were already occupied by identifiable owners, such as the Maoris in New Zealand or the Zulus in Natal. In either case the whites displaced the indigenous people and reduced their status to that of primitive intruders, to be isolated in 'reservations' in the backlands.

A second form of imperial expansion was directed not towards acquiring lands for settlement but towards capturing markets and securing important natural resources for exploitation. These mainly sub-tropical colonies began with the seizure of the Spice Islands of South-east Asia in the seventeenth century and with the search for El Dorado, the Land of Gold, in South America. Sugar, cotton and tobacco were the main products in the eighteenth century. The nineteenth century saw the development of tea, cocoa, rubber, tin and other minerals in tropical lands. All these manufactures required large numbers of cheap workers, employed on a permanent basis. Finally, as we noted, the tropical world was carved up because it was Manifest Destiny to do so.

These different forms of colonialism entailed different kinds of treatment for the 'lesser breeds without the law', but in every case black and brown people were treated as separate and unequal. There were the colonies which the whites regarded as wholly their domain. Most were within the British Empire: Australia, Canada and New Zealand. The United States was a white-Protestant domain, despite the many minorities who were neither Protestant nor (in the Anglo-Saxon's terms) white: and the United States should be regarded as a vast internal empire. Similarly, Russian expansion created a vast hinterland which was as much an imperial backyard as the prairies of North America. A colony was not, necessarily, a territory gained by expeditions across the seas.

To begin with the most familiar form of colonial settlement – the peopling of Australia, New Zealand and Canada – we discover that an early feature of social and economic development is a tussle between the minority who try to recreate the social order of Europe, with the landed magnate as the dominant element, and the majority who are determined to create an entirely different social order, with the independent working farmer as the essential element in the social framework. The landlords wanted to import landless labourers to work their estates; the farmers wanted to restrict immigration to settlers of their own type. As these colonies became urbanised and industrialised the clash of interests became even more direct. The skilled and semi-skilled urban workers were determined to exclude any who might dilute the labour force, thus giving more power to the bosses who could then depress wages and extend hours of work.

The colonial landlords sought to augment their labour supply by introducing workers who were not free to quit. In the seventeenth and eighteenth centuries, many of the inhabitants of the British Isles were compulsorily consigned to North America; some were virtually political exiles – the supporters of Monmouth's rebellion, or Highlanders captured after the 'Forty-Five'. More were felons, convicted of a criminal offence and transported. After American independence, convicts were transported to Australia where they helped to open up the new sheeplands. In 1845 and 1849, the inhabitants of Melbourne forcibly prevented the landing of convicts. The whole system of transportation was abolished in 1867. This was not enough for the Australians. Several colonies passed laws excluding poor persons from being 'dumped' in their land, while more stringent sanctions were taken to exclude non-whites who, it was argued, would depress the living standards of Australia and, equally important, damage its way of life.

The first moves to keep Asians out of Australia came in the 1850s when the goldfields of Victoria attracted large numbers of Chinese diggers. The Victoria legislature passed an Act to exclude the Chinese in 1855, though the Australians were reluctant to introduce laws which were openly racist in character. And so restrictions were placed on the numbers which passenger ships might carry, while all immigrants had to pay an entry tax of £10. To evade these restrictions, Chinese were landed in South Australia and made their way into Victoria overland. By 1859 there were 42,000 Chinese in the goldfields, but then the boom subsided and so did the immigration (by 1890 there were less than 36,000 Chinese in Australia). Various measures restricting Asian immigration were enacted but were refused the royal assent in London. Meanwhile, a much greater Chinese migration was developing on the west coast of North America. Thousands were imported as labourers, in what was inelegantly termed the 'pig trade', to build roads and railways: by 1880 there were about 105,000 Chinese in the U.S.A. As the white population of California, Washington State and British Columbia expanded, so did antipathy to Chinese competition. In 1882 the United States Congress passed the Chinese Exclusion Act, barring all further immigration (and at the same time excluding paupers and criminals). Canada followed suit in 1885 with 'an Act to restrict and regulate Chinese immigration into Canada', and this was not denied the royal assent.

The 1880s were marked by declarations of explicitly racist doctrines in all the new, white countries. In Australia, the Prime Minister of Victoria, D. Gillies, declared: 'They [the Chinese] are not only an alien race, but they remain aliens. Thus, we have not a colonization in any true sense of the word but practically a sort of powerful invasion of our land by Chinese', while the Prime Minister of New South Wales, Sir Henry Parkes, corroborated this thinking: 'I believe the Chinese to be a powerful race, capable of taking a great hold upon my country, and because I wish to preserve the type of my own nation . . . I am, and always have been, opposed to the influx of Chinese.' The Labour leader, William Lane, summed it all up: 'The blacks on our plantations, the lascars on our coasts, the Chinese in our towns and on our squattages all threaten the life of White Australia. Unless Australia is to be white, what does it matter to us what becomes of it?'

And so Sir Charles Dilke, the English aristocrat who roughed it in Australia and America, discovered: 'The colonial workman does not look with favour upon the dark-skinned labourer, and the Chinaman – of whom he has seen something – he distinctly hates'.[2] New Zealand followed the prevailing pattern by enacting an Asiatic Restriction Bill 'to safeguard the race purity of the people of New Zealand'; this was disallowed in London, but in its place there was brought forward an Immigration Restriction Bill modelled upon the

Natal Immigration Act, 1897, which allowed immigration officers to exclude any person who was unable to write a declaration in a prescribed European language.[3] The provision did not apply to those arriving from Britain. This literacy test received the royal assent in 1900, and provided a model adopted by Australia and Canada in their policy of keeping out non-whites. All whom it was intended to exclude could easily be excluded (Australian immigration officers sometimes tested the new arrival's proficiency in the Irish language), while it was possible to pretend that there was no ban based upon people's skin-colour or race.

Following the exclusion of the Chinese from the United States many Japanese took their place, entering California as craftsmen, market gardeners (or truck farmers), fishermen, houseboys, etc. Although no ban was imposed on their entry they were treated as transients, not immigrants. Japanese (and other Asians) could not qualify for citizenship: though their children born in America (the *Nisei*) had to be accepted as citizens. Japanese could not own property, and therefore at law remained employees only. In the early 1900s, when a new generation of American-born Japanese began to grow up, they were excluded from the Californian school system and accommodated in separate, oriental schools.

Japanese prestige was high at this time, after the war with Russia, and the Japanese government protested to President Theodore Roosevelt against the separate schools; Roosevelt thereafter concluded a 'gentleman's agreement' with Japan, whereby in return for admission to the Californian schools, the Japanese government undertook to refuse the issue of passports to all would-be emigrants to America. Thereafter, the flow of Japanese entering California dwindled to a trickle. Despite the 'gentleman's agreement', those already living in America continued to be subject to discrimination: not merely in social terms (refusal to sell houses to Japanese, for example) but also by legal discrimination; the *Nisei* were not admitted to the electoral register if they failed to pass the English test, while in 1911 the Bureau of Naturalisation ruled that Japanese, and all other 'Orientals' were ineligible for citizenship, which was admissible only to white (Caucasian) and Negro immigrants. Some Japanese unsuccessfully contested this ruling on the ground that they were descended from the Ainu, the autochthonous inhabitants of Japan, who (it was argued) were not of Mongolian stock. Just like the blacks of the South, the Chinese or Japanese who wanted to 'make it' had somehow to 'pass for white'.

Canada also applied exclusionist policies against immigrants from British India (locally termed 'Hindus' to distinguish them from Canada's own indigenous Indians). Most of these immigrants were Sikh ex-soldiers of the Indian Army: tough, adventurous men, who worked as lumberjacks and helped to build the trans-Canada railroad. From about 1908, because of white opposition, they were excluded by an ingenious regulation which laid down that all immigrants must travel from their country of origin by one continuous journey – and this was not possible from India to Canada. When a Sikh businessman sought to meet the rules by chartering the Japanese ship *Komagata Maru* from Calcutta to Vancouver, the passengers were forbidden to land, and the ship had to take them home again. In consequence, the 'Hindu' community in British Columbia remained small, and even those born in Canada were denied civil rights – they could not vote or serve upon juries.

Immigration into the United States was even more hazardous for those denounced as the 'turbaned tide'. In 1907 there were riots in Seattle and other towns in Washington State against the Indians (most of whom had arrived via Canada), and they were forcibly expelled by anti-Asian groups. An Asiatic Exclusion League was a major force in Californian politics, campaigning against the admission of all Asians, 1907 – 13.[4] Finally the Immigration Act of 1917 banned the entry of all Asians, except Japanese, into the U.S.A. They became liable to imprisonment and expulsion. Fewer than two thousand remained. The most acceptable were the small numbers of Indian mystics, the 'swamis', who joined California's medley of eclectic religions. Like the Japanese, some Indians tried to overcome America's discriminatory regulations by pleading that they were Aryans, and really Caucasians. Their attempt to 'pass for white' was equally unsuccessful. Even the most eminent visiting Indians experienced discrimination. When the poet Rabindranath Tagore entered the United States from Canada in 1929 he was so disgusted by the treatment he received from immigration officials that he cancelled his lecture tour and returned to India immediately.

This unilateral exclusion of the ancient nations of Asia – China, Japan and India – by the new, white nations was a clear demonstration of the division of the world on racial lines which was increasingly resented by all who were black and brown. The statesmen of the British Empire who gathered for Queen Victoria's Diamond Jubilee heard Joseph Chamberlain speak of 'the traditions of the Empire which makes no distinction in favour of, or against, race or colour', while in the same breath he exclaimed 'We quite sympathise with the determination of the white inhabitants of these [self-governing] colonies . . . that there should not be an influx of people alien in civilisation, alien in religion, alien in custom.' What was gratifying to the Australian listener was humiliating to the Indian. And with what disillusionment would an Asian visitor to New York scan the Statue of Liberty with its inscription:

> Give me your tired, your poor,
> Your huddled masses, yearning to breathe free

— but not your Chinese poor or your huddled Japanese yearning to breathe free.

Sir Charles Dilke described with a radical's sympathy the labour movements in Australia, New Zealand and other White Dominions; but he felt compelled to add: 'It is a curious fact that the English race have more generally destroyed the native races with which they have come in contact in their young settlements than has been the case with other colonising peoples, but have destroyed the natives only afterwards to enter into a conflict with other dark or yellow races.' After surveying the history of the American Indian, the Australian bushman, the Maori and the autochthonous Africans of Cape Colony in South Africa, Dilke added: 'South Africa . . . has in some parts replaced them by an even greater number of dark-skinned people — coloured immigrants of another kind are pouring in from across the seas as labourers.' He was discussing the second type of colonial situation in which a settler or planter class of whites demanded the right to import labour for their estates, or their mines, because the sons of the soil were not available to provide a labour force.

After the abolition of the slave trade (followed by the abolition of slavery itself) the great reservoir of black servile labour was no longer automatically available.* Attempts were made to find cheap labour for sub-tropical plantations from West Africa, from Portugal and other lands facing the Atlantic, but these supplies were insufficient. The planters turned to those two great reservoirs of manpower, China and India. We have seen that these peoples were rejected as emigrants into

---

* Slavery ended in the British Empire in 1834, and in the French Empire in 1848. However, France continued with a system of virtual slavery – the *engagés forcés*, until 1872. Slavery was abolished in the United States in 1865, and slaves in the Dutch Empire were liberated in 1870. Spain abolished slavery in Puerto Rico in 1872, but it continued in Cuba until the American occupation in 1898. Brazil finally abolished slavery in 1888. Thus, in the 1970s, there are many black people whose fathers were slaves.

the temperate lands, but there was an almost insatiable demand for them in the plantation colonies. The Chinese were exported from the southern ports – Canton, Macao and Hong Kong. Most went under a bond of indenture whereby they agreed to serve for five or seven years at a stipulated wage. Some had no agreement and virtually sold themselves for a few dollars to an agent, who sold them to an employer in the new country.[5] Because the demand was for manual workers, the 'pig trade' dealt almost exclusively in Chinese males: virtually no women were exported. When they arrived at their destination, the Chinese were worked to exhaustion like slaves and most failed to return to China. A few managed to get out of the estates and set up petty stores; they married any woman they could find – black or white. In consequence, this Chinese emigration, numbered in many millions, often led to no permanent Chinese settlement. In Cuba, Jamaica and Guiana few survived to perpetuate themselves through descendants. They died and were forgotten.

In countries nearer to China the emigration was less vicious, and many more survived to become settlers. The 'Southern Seas', the *Nanyang* – which today we call South-east Asia – was an area which workers from south China could reach on their own initiative. Most had to borrow to make the journey and were compelled to work under a labour contractor, the *Kapitan China*. Most eventually freed themselves from servile labour and by membership of the secret societies, the *Hui* or *Kongsi* (the most famous being the Triad or Three-world Society), they obtained protection and support in launching out into trade and manufacture.

Only less numerous than the Chinese were the Indian emigrants, who were also exported under indenture, binding themselves to work for one employer for a minimum of five years. Because they were subjects of British India a much more systematic attempt was made to secure some elementary rights for them. Thus, they were shipped through government emigration depots at Calcutta and Madras in special vessels carrying government-appointed surgeon-supervisors. On arrival, they came under the surveillance of an official termed the protector of immigrants. However, the elaborate rules were frequently evaded. Thus, it was provided that every hundred men must be accompanied by twenty-five women to preserve some semblance of a normal society, but this proportion was hardly ever fulfilled.[6]

On the plantations, whether the product was sugar, coffee, tea, rubber or tobacco, the power structure was almost always the same. At the apex was the planter, who was always a European (British, French, Dutch) and who was absolute ruler of his petty kingdom. He had assistants, sometimes called overseers, who might also be young Europeans, or men of mixed origin – Eurasians or Mestizos – who carried out the planter's orders but also carried an air of authority (they were usually on horseback). The plantation would be organised by sections: a number of fields, or a particular process, would be under the supervision of a foreman or ganger, called the 'driver'. In the days of slavery he had been the slave-driver; now he became the coolie-driver, and it was his job to get the maximum amount of work from his gang, ensuring that each worker attained a stipulated norm, called the 'task'. The driver, the lowest member of the hierarchy of authority, was a promoted coolie, Indian or Chinese, like his gang.

The planter, whether he was the proprietor of the estate or a manager, liked to appear above the daily toil of the workers. His word was law, to punish or (very rarely) to reward. A good planter liked to preside over the social and family life of the estate, as well as its working existence. He patronised the annual festivals; he adjudicated in disputes. There is an Indian term, *Mai-Bap*, 'Mother-Father', which the planter liked to be accorded. His paternalism brooked no questioning; he fixed the rates of pay and the hours of work; he decreed when there might be a holiday; he punished the idle or miscreant employee. Very often he was the father of his workers (or some of them) in a literal sense; but he never forgot that it was for the white to give the orders and for the black or brown to obey.

The planters formed a tightly knit community, very conscious that they had to defend the interests of their class against the demands of the workers, the criticism of humanitarian and reformist circles in the metropolitan country, and the interference of the colonial government. The workers were helpless, and could be disciplined if they protested; the critics were far away and powerless to intervene, and the colonial authorities hesitated and were reluctant to confront the most powerful economic force in the territory. Life could be made very unpleasant for a colonial governor who tried to move against the planters. One British governor who exposed the tyranny of the planters, Sir Arthur Gordon (Lord Stanmore), told a commission of inquiry: 'Where the employers of labour form . . . the whole of the upper class of society and influence every other class, it requires a very great deal of courage . . . to stand up against that influence.'

In Malaya or Guiana, the British planter was usually the manager on behalf of a company, serving in the country for twenty or thirty years and dreaming all the time of retirement in Bournemouth or Wimbledon. But in many colonies the white planters became a permanently domiciled community, virtually a master race. In the Dutch East Indies, the Dutch who ran the sugar, rubber and other plantations remained from generation to generation. Those who returned to the Netherlands for retirement were called *Trekkers*, those permanently domiciled were called *Blijvers* or Belongers. It was the same with the French planters in Indo-China and Algeria and the white French population of the sugar colonies in the Caribbean and the Indian Ocean. For these domiciled French a special term was coined: that of Creole.* Similarly, in Hawaii a permanent white planting aristocracy evolved out of the sons of American missionaries who acquired plantations from the kings and queens of Hawaii.

The nearest British equivalent to these communities of Creoles emerged in the temperate and highland zones of Africa. A strange feature of Victorian and Edwardian social life was the manner in which the upper classes got rid of the misfits, the failures, the shady characters to the colonies, in the belief that (like Mr Micawber in fiction) they would become new men in the new environment. Some of these gentry found their way to Kenya and to Rhodesia, as well as to Natal in South Africa (see Map 1). They acquired huge estates in the pioneer days when legal ownership was hazy both under African and British systems of law. In Kenya the leader was Lord Delamere, who in the twentieth century achieved the same takeover of vast areas as the aristocrats of the seventeenth century had done in North America. Most of those who settled on the land were soldiers of fortune, adventurers, but they imitated the few genuine aristocrats in establishing a spacious style of living which was an anachronism in the twentieth century, made possible by control over the sources of cheap labour.

All these planter regimes – Dutch, French, American, British – reinforced their privileged position by laws and rules to prevent anyone of another race from gaining entry into their exclusive order. In Kenya the white settlers settled the issue once and for all when they succeeded in their claim that the Highlands, the most fertile and climatically agreeable portion of Kenya, should be reserved exclusively for the white farmers. Thus an area of nearly 17,000 square miles was

---

* The word originally meant a plant, transplanted and acclimatised in the tropics. Perhaps the most famous Creole was Joséphine de Beauharnais, Napoleon's first wife.

declared closed to those who had been its previous inhabitants, the African tribe of the Kikuyu. They could dwell there only as the labourers and servants of the whites. The alienation of African lands was equally ruthless in Rhodesia; while in South Africa the whites claimed all the land except for the barren backlands preserved as African reservations.

Everywhere, the planters aimed to create laws and regulations which would impose penal conditions of labour upon the indigenous people, enforceable by the police and magistrates through fines and sentence of imprisonment. As far as possible they tried to fill the ranks of the civil service, judiciary and the security forces with their own white Creole people instead of officials from the *métropole* who might have a sentimental sympathy for 'native interests'. The justification for white privilege was usually that the settlers, the *colons*, were preserving the 'Englishness' or the 'Frenchness' or the Dutch or American character of their portion of Africa, Asia or the Pacific. There was a relentless insistence that it was the British, French or some other white pioneers who had opened up an area previously backward or barbarous. It was European pluck, determination, skill, inventiveness, which had introduced the blessings of sugar, tea, rubber or another extractive cultivation. It was European civilisation which bestowed peace and order on societies torn by feuding and anarchy. They insisted that to hand over even tiny portions of responsibility to any outside the white circle was to risk a return to anarchy.

The white settlers claimed to represent Britain and British values in the face of sporadic attempts from the centre to liberalise the Empire and extend the rights of British citizenship to the 'lesser breeds'. In Kenya there was a British government proposal to admit some of the most educated, prosperous members of the Indian community to the franchise. The whites responded by preparing a plan to take over the colony and expel the Indians to the coast. Confronted by the prospect of rebellion, the Colonial Secretary, Lord Devonshire, advised the Cabinet that the introduction of British military forces to subdue the 9000 white settler rebels 'is in my opinion out of the question'. He advised concessions to the whites. Kenya had to wait nearly forty years (that is from then, 1923, until 1960) before non-whites were admitted to any share in the process of government.[7] (The reaction of the Conservative government of 1923 was almost exactly akin to the reaction of the Labour government in 1965 when confronted with white rebellion in Rhodesia.)

There were colonies, especially in Africa, which were unsuitable for any form of white settlement. Far into the twentieth century West Africa was called 'the white man's grave'. These areas were annexed for strategic reasons – by the British to keep out the French, or vice versa – or because European missionaries had demanded annexation as protection against persecution, as in Uganda (or Vietnam). These countries had a rather low place in the calculations of imperialism; as Gunnar Myrdal writes:

The peoples in the colonies were assumed to be differently constituted from people of White European stock. They lacked interest in improving their lot. This theory was given learned expression by the economists in the so-called backward sloping supply curve. It was underpinned by observations of their different cultural traditions, attitudes and institutions. The hot damp climate . . . was also given an important role. At the basis, though often carefully concealed, was the racial inferiority doctrine.[8]

All this scarcely connected up with the democratic ideas which steadily changed the society of the West in the late nineteenth and early twentieth centuries. In the West, the belief in an aristocracy, born to rule, was fast disappearing from the sphere of politics, though still firmly entrenched in important parts of the economic sphere. The cult of empire clashed with the cult of the common man. Occasionally these competing ideas and principles came into conflict.[9] King Leopold of Belgium managed the basin of the river Congo as his own private estate, extracting its natural wealth through Belgian cartels with monopoly privileges (see Map 1). Largely through investigations by E. D. Morel, a Socialist Internationalist, and Roger Casement, then British Consul at Boma, the existence of systematic methods of torture to extract a wide range of natural products was brought to the world's notice. The subsequent outcry compelled the Belgian government to take over the responsibility of administering the Congo.

A different kind of scandal was exposed in South Africa, when in order to meet a labour shortage in the mines of the Rand the British government sanctioned the importation of 47,000 Chinese workers. This 'Chinese slavery' was a major issue in the British general election of 1906, and played a part in the downfall of the Conservatives. However, perhaps the reason why British working men turned against the Tories was because they supposed that the Chinese were taking away the employment of white men. Graham Wallas, who observed the election closely, recorded: 'The pictures of Chinamen on the hoardings aroused among many of the voters an immediate hatred of the Mongolian racial type. This hatred was transferred to the Conservative Party.'[10]

The political philosophy of the British Empire was to move from centralised control by London towards 'responsible government': that is self-government, later defined as 'Dominion Status'. The Dominion of Canada was launched with the federation agreement of 1867; a similar federation brought together the Australian colonies in the Commonwealth of Australia in 1901, while in 1910 the former Boer republics and British colonies in South Africa achieved full self-government as the Union of South Africa. In Canada and Australia the new nations were also white nations (apart from the remnants of the indigenous races), but in South Africa the whites were outnumbered by the blacks in the ratio 4:1. How far were the blacks consulted in the transfer of power? The answer, of course, is that they were not consulted at all. There were a few black and coloured voters in Cape Colony, and after Union they retained the franchise; in British Natal the Indians had already been removed from the voting register, and in the Transvaal and the Orange Free State non-whites had never enjoyed the vote, or any other civil rights. President Kruger had insisted that being the sons of Ham it was God's Will that they serve their white masters for all eternity. During negotiations for the new Union the Liberal government in Britain never considered the future of blacks or coloureds or Indians in a South Africa governed by the whites. Their only concern was to carry through a reform which, they believed, would ensure responsible government by English-speaking South Africans and prevent a Boer resurgence. They were astonished when Botha and Smuts, the Boer leaders, gained a majority. The reason was that some British voters in the Transvaal responded to their appeal to enforce restrictions against the non-whites.

The whole future direction of the British Empire came up for questioning when, in 1917, the British government announced that India's constitutional progress was in the direction of responsible government. For the first time it was formally accepted that a non-white people must be regarded as equal to the white member-states of the Empire. The British government, and especially the Liberal Secretary of State for India, was prepared to recognise India's new status, and gave this a symbolic significance by insisting upon India's signature to the Treaty of Versailles and by claiming Indian membership in the new League of Nations. The existing Dominions were less enthusiastic. All possessed immigration laws which barred the entry of Indians.

However, at the Imperial Conference of 1921 Canada, Australia and New Zealand assented to a declaration that there was an 'incongruity' between India being an equal member of the British Empire and 'the existence of disabilities upon British Indians lawfully domiciled in some other parts of the Empire'. South Africa (represented by Smuts) refused to agree to this declaration.[11]

In 1921, Britain recognised the Irish claim to freedom and the Irish Free State was born; Southern Rhodesia with its tiny white minority received a form of self-government in 1923 which ended all but the last vestiges of control by London. But India's demand for full self-government (*Purna Swaraj*) had to be satisfied with a halfway house called dyarchy, in which the functions of government were divided between an official ('reserved') half and an elected, ministerial ('transferred') half. When it was announced that further reform would be subject to a favourable report by a British parliamentary commission, Indian political leaders were furious. The moderate father of a socialist son, Motilal Nehru, speculated on the assessment to be made by this commission in a speech to the legislature in New Delhi:

What is the state of education in India? What progress have representative institutions made? Whether these people deserve any further progress or whether it is necessary to send them down a form or two to learn their lessons better . . . ? Now, that is the sort of thing we are objecting to. We say we are absolutely fit for self-government, as fit as you are in your own island. This is what we say. Here we are occupying that position and you tell us as you would tell school-boys: be good boys and you will be promoted to a higher form.[12]

Between the two world wars there was no further move towards broadening the British Empire from a 'white man's club' into a multi-racial club. The 1920s and 1930s were the high noon of the Empire when the brotherhood of the white member countries was replenished by a great movement of emigrants from Britain to the White Dominions. Whereas in the nineteenth century 70 per cent of British emigrants headed towards the United States and 10 per cent to Canada, in the 1920s only 18 per cent went to the United States while 45 per cent headed for Canada and 30 per cent for Australia. This was despite the action of the United States in 1924 in introducing a quota system whereby the 'lesser breeds' of Europe were severely restricted and British immigrants were massively favoured by a selection system which emphasised 'Nordic superiority'.*

* Under the 1924 Act, immigration quotas were related to the ethnic composition of

It was the movement of emigrants from Britain into the White Commonwealth which attracted attention; the settlement of hundreds of thousands of Indians in Ceylon and South-east Asia in the same years passed unnoticed by British statesmen. During the 1930s, because of the world depression, many British emigrants returned to the United Kingdom. However, the Second World War with its massive shaking up of peoples seemed to anticipate another great emigration, and the Duke of Devonshire (whose father acquiesced in white defiance in the 1920s) declared on behalf of the British government (1943) that migration was mainly the concern of the receiving country: 'It is quite clearly for any country to decide on which terms persons from other countries are to enter and to settle.'[13] This confirmed the constitutional conception of the British Commonwealth as a community of white, British, self-governing (or independent) countries looking to Britain for a lead, but determining their own policies entirely on their own.

The transformation of the White Dominions into fully self-governing entities, and the prolonged discussion about how India might, through intermediary stages, attain Dominion Status had no counterpart in the French Empire. France had expanded its conquests in Africa and elsewhere very largely in compensation for defeat by Germany in 1870 and the loss of Alsace – Lorraine. The French Empire was regarded as a valuable property and the free-trade philosophy which was accepted doctrine in nineteenth-century Britain was confronted by the French doctrine of *mise en valeur*, or colonial protection. At an earlier stage, French policy was declared to be that of *assimilation*. Algeria, with its French settlers, the *pieds noirs*, became an extension of France, with its own *départements*, electing deputies to the Assembly in Paris. Subsequently, French policy became that of *association*, which meant that the colonial territories forever remained subordinate to the Ministry of the Colonies. The colonial peoples had the status not of *citoyen* but of *sujet*, liable to compulsory labour service and military conscription. True, a number of advisory councils were established in the French colonies but these were dominated by the *colons*. The status of *citoyen* could be attained by a small minority of the colonial population, the intelligentsia, those with a French secondary-school certificate and

---

the United States in 1920. Thus, 41·4 per cent of the quota was reserved for immigrants from Great Britain: in no year was this quota taken up. By contrast, Italians only received 3 per cent of the quota and Greeks 2 per cent. Lists of applicants from these countries stretched ahead for years (in 1960, 265,773 Italians waited for entry in the Italian quota of 5666). Asia received no quota at all.

those who advanced in the administration; but this status had to be acquired by an elaborate process of naturalisation. Perhaps because they valued the privilege so highly, these black and brown Frenchmen were, in general, intensely loyal to France and French culture. For example, Félix Houphouet-Boigny, President of the Ivory Coast Republic, was a deputy in the French Assembly and a member of the French Cabinet. Léopold Senghor, the Poet – President of Senegal – progenitor of the concept of *négritude* – became a member of the French Academy in 1969, the first African member.

German colonialism lasted a bare thirty years (1885–1914) and was stamped with efficient organisation at its best and ruthless repression at its worst. When in South West Africa (Namibia) the Herero tribe rose in rebellion in protest against the seizure of their lands, the German general, Von Trotha, issued orders for their total extermination (see Map 1). Humanitarian protest in Germany caused the Kaiser to countermand the order: but not before 75,000 Hereros had been wiped out. Perhaps the prevailing colonial philosophy is best illustrated by an edict issued by the *Deutsche Kolonialbund*: 'In Court, the evidence of one white man can only be outweighed by the evidence of seven coloured persons.'

The last Dutch governor-general of the Indonesian archipelago affirmed that the Indies had been Dutch for three hundred years and would be Dutch for three hundred more. Although policies might change, the Indies were essentially a Dutch possession. From 1920, the constitution declared that the Indies formed an integral part of the Dutch kingdom. A People's Council, or *Volksraad*, was established, but of its fifty-five members twenty-five were Netherlanders. The use of the word 'Indonesia' was forbidden by law.

While in Britain, France and the Netherlands there was still some debate about the future of the colonies, the lands into which the Europeans had first expanded – those conquered by the Portuguese – remained cocooned in their own beliefs about themselves; beliefs that assumed that they had resolved the relations between the different races by assimilating all into the Iberian, Portuguese civilisation. This belief was at its strongest in Brazil, which formally separated from Portugal in 1822. Because tiny Portugal could only send small numbers of soldiers and sailors to the overseas possessions they were encouraged, from the start, to cohabit or marry with local women, and their children were brought up as Catholics and Portuguese. Millions of slaves were imported into Brazil from Africa, and the Portuguese planters and ranchers took the women for themselves. In Brazil and in the Portuguese African possessions it was quite possible for a slave to purchase his freedom. Thus societies evolved in which the lowest strata were black, *negro*, those at the top were white, *blanco*, and a vast intermediate group were mixed, *mulatto* or *mestizo*. (A saying often quoted in former days was that 'Brazil is a Hell for Negroes, a Purgatory for whites and a Paradise for mulattoes'.) Because there was no fixed line drawn between the groups, the Portuguese declared that there was no colour bar as in American or British colonial societies. Because all were Portuguese there was no question of metropolitan or colonial separatism: and indeed a vast outward emigration of poor peasants continued in the twentieth century to Brazil and to Angola and Mozambique together with a smaller inward immigration from these settlements to Portugal. The supposed success of the *assimilado* philosophy was invoked as a reason for leaving things alone: the first civil rights Act in Brazil was only passed in 1950.

Confronting these confident creeds of paternalistic Western control there was the anti-colonial political philosophy of the United States. It was true that the United States had annexed islands in the Pacific, such as Hawai and Samoa, and had taken possession of the remnant of the great Spanish Empire of former days – Puerto Rico, Guam and the Philippines. Cuba was not formally annexed, but the island was virtually an American protectorate, with a massive military and naval base of Guantanamo Bay (which is still [1976] retained, despite Fidel Castro). It was proclaimed that all this was fulfilling Divine Providence: it was Manifest Destiny. Yet this new American empire was somehow supposed to be different; 'Big Brother' (for the term was seriously invoked) was to help the 'Little brown Brother' to learn how to be free. It was somehow irrelevant that the American army was compelled to wage a long-drawn-out war against the Filipino guerillas before that country could be introduced to the blessings of democracy. It was also somehow irrelevant that the United States Marines were despatched to occupy sovereign black and brown states in the Caribbean, in some cases for twenty years or more.* As one still widely used American college textbook observes: 'The islanders badly needed tutelage and

* The United States occupied Panama, 1903–18, subsequently pulling back into the Canal Zone. In Mexico, the port of Vera Cruz was occupied in 1914, while the U.S.A. went to war with Mexico, 1916–17. Nicaragua was occupied by the Marines, 1912–33, and Haiti from 1915–34. Dominica was occupied twice, 1916–24, and 1965–66. Guatemala was occupied in 1954.

preparation for self-government.'[14] From Woodrow Wilson to Franklin D. Roosevelt, American policy was based upon the principle that the United States was not like other imperial powers.

Wilsonian idealism was given expression in the League of Nations, which was itself an instrument for perpetuating international white racialism rather than a move against racialism and colonialism. The philosophy of the League was expressed in its charter or Covenant, and when this was discussed Japan demanded that there should be a provision for the abolition of racial discrimination. Primarily, the Japanese were aiming at the discriminatory immigration laws of the United States and Wilson was put in a dilemma: the League, his own brainchild, was unpopular with the United States Congress and he could not hope to gain acceptance for what Harold Nicolson described as 'so dangerous a principle as the equality of the yellow man with the white man, [which] might even imply the terrific theory of the equality of the white man with the black'. Fortunately, Billy Hughes, the tough little Prime Minister of Australia, saved the day. Even less than the United States could Australia accede to a demand which would open its doors to the Yellow Peril; Hughes dismissed the Japanese proposal as nonsense. The Covenant bypassed the proposition that all men are created equal.[15]

Woodrow Wilson hoped to employ the downfall of the German and Turkish empires as the basis for a more general reduction of imperialism. The League of Nations was given responsibility for administering the former German and Turkish possessions under a Mandates Commission. In actuality, the particular power which had wrested a territory from the enemy was in every case entrusted with the mandate for that territory: the German Cameroons went to France, German South West Africa to South Africa, Tanganyika to Britain, and Rwanda—Burundi to Belgium. All these territories became 'C Class' mandates, and were indistinguishable from colonies, for they were administered without any participation by their own peoples in their government. However, in conformity with the innate racial attitudes of the time, the Arab countries, along with Lebanon and Palestine (formerly under Turkish rule), as the heirs to the ancient Semitic civilisation, were regarded as potentially ready for self-government. The 'A Class' mandates allotted to France and Britain were more like protectorates, and representatives of the old Arab and Christian élite were included in the upper levels of administration.

The League of Nations also staked an interest in the colonial field with its International Labour Office (I.L.O.), founded in 1919. The I.L.O. was mainly concerned with industrial welfare in the West, but it developed a minor concern for plantation labour, and for different kinds of forced labour, still widely practised in tropical colonies. Lacking any power of intervention, the I.L.O. could do no more than occasionally call for reports.

The League of Nations did include a few non-Western countries; in Africa there were Liberia and Ethiopia, while in Asia, India, China, Japan and Siam (Thailand) were members. However, the League was virtually a European club, and because the United States did not join, and the Soviet Union was not a member for very long, it was dominated by Britain and France. It was largely the ineffectiveness of the League in conflicts outside Europe, however, which brought it into disrepute. Japan's invasion of China elicited only the most feeble response, and Japanese representatives shouted derision at the impotent League Assembly. The Italian invasion of Ethiopia did, belatedly, lead to the enforcement of economic sanctions (though not over the supply of oil).

The imperial high noon radiated out in lands which were, formally, not colonial territories at all. Empires do not have to be external; and in the first part of the twentieth century the subjugation of the 'lesser breeds' was ultimately most effective in North America – the Land of the Free – in Australia, and perhaps most of all in the non-Russian territories of the Soviet Union.

There has been a remarkable similarity in the treatment of the indigenous peoples by their white successors everywhere. In North America, South Africa and Australia the whites encountered peoples with strong tribal organisations, mainly nomadic, with an economy based upon hunting and herding. In the first phase, the whites treated more or less equally with the Amerindians and others, concluding agreements and purchasing land, even though for purely nominal values. As they became stronger, the whites pushed the indigenous people back, out of what were now their colonies, and when they were challenged the whites attacked with all the weapons of modern warfare. Finally, the indigenous tribes were restricted to reservations and were given a separate status as non-citizens and in many respects non-humans. Their meagre privileges were further restricted when 'native' territory was found to possess mineral or other resources, and the doles dispensed to the tribes were subject to their observing good behaviour: that is, staying on the reservations and obeying the white man.

The total Amerindian population on the eve of European colonisation was about 15 million, according to the most cautious estimates.[16] Over one million of them lived north of the Rio Grande (that is, in the present territory of the U.S.A. and Canada). By the end of the nineteenth century the number of northern Amerindians had fallen to less than a quarter of a million, as a result of warfare, pestilence and starvation. In the following fifty years the number rose to more than half a million, with 155, 874 recorded in Canada and 455,500 in the United States (1951). Many more had moved off the reservations and thereby forfeited their small privileges: in Canada these people are called *métis* (mixed) and their numbers are as many as those of the 'status' Indians. Down to the Second World War, the Amerindians were denied equal civil rights with the general population and were still being squeezed out of their land. Government dealt with them through a special (white) Indian administration. The circumstances of the Australian Bushman were similar, though their extinction was even more complete. The Zulus and other tribes in South Africa were also excluded from most of the lands which had once been their own. All except the most barren backlands were declared to be 'white man's country'.

The internal empire which gripped the black man in the American South was established not by physically isolating the Negro but by systematically depriving him of any share in the privileges reserved for the whites. With the reclamation of the South into the Union there followed in the 1870s the period of 'reconstruction' in which, under Federal supervision, the Negroes obtained citizenship rights, including participation in government at the state level. Yet, after Federal troops were withdrawn, the southern whites succeeded in re-establishing an ascendancy almost as total as they had enjoyed when slave-owners. The main weapon was intimidation, though full use was also made of the Negro's ignorance and economic weakness. Between 1870 and 1900, the American Negro was deprived of the vote by exclusive voter registration laws; he was excluded from juries and from all public offices, and he was required to accept separate institutions, both public and private. Blacks had separate schools, separate hospitals, separate cemeteries, and were required to eat in separate hotels and travel in separate railway carriages and separate sections on the buses.

Attempts were made to appeal to Washington over the heads of county judges and state governors: for emancipation had come only from Washington. Yet, in a series of judgements stretching over seventy years, from 1883 to 1954, the Supreme Court dismissed all attempts to reassert black rights. The Supreme Court declared that it was powerless to intervene, even when the southern whites went outside the law, as in attempts to make Washington take note of the lynchings which were the South's ultimate weapon. The Supreme Court declined to intervene when white racist laws invaded private life — as in forbidding marriage between different races in Mississippi and other states — thus depriving itself of its proper constitutional power of intervening in the segregationist debate. Not until the Supreme Court's decision in 1954 in the case of *Brown* v. *Board of Education*, which reversed the decisions of its predecessors, did Washington attempt to moderate the southern whites' assertion of supremacy over their black empire.

Imperial Russia, and then the U.S.S.R., also imposed a total system of control upon all the non-Russian peoples. Those who may be described as 'ethnic' Russians form over half the total population (58 per cent in 1939; 54 per cent in 1949 after the annexation of the Baltic states and parts of Poland, Finland and Romania). The Ukrainians are the second group — less than one-fifth of the total — and the non-European peoples form only small and fragmented minorities.* Imperial Russia treated the non-European territories as a land of conquest, and a city such as Tashkent consisted of a modern Western, Russian garrison-town or cantonment and a 'native' city in which the traditional layout was unchanged and where Islamic, traditional values survived. A few members of the Central Asian aristocracy (like General Alikhanov) were assimilated and thoroughly russified. The remainder were left in a 'fossil' condition, like the Amerindians.

The Soviet constitution, in theory, recognises the existence of separate nationalities, and a number of national republics came into being in the Caucasus (e.g. Georgia, Armenia, Azerbaidzhan, Dagestan) and in Central Asia. As in the rest of the U.S.S.R. the Communist Party is the only political organisation and the political élite have been totally assimilated to the Russian, Stalinist mode. Education is almost wholly through the medium of Russian, and there is a steady expansion of the Russian language at the expense of all the others: by 1970, Russian had become the language of 80 per cent of the population (the 1970 Census listed 108 ethnic groups, most with their own languages).

---

* Uzbeks over 9 million; Tartars nearly 6 million; Kazakhs over 5 million; Azerbaidzhanis, Armenians, Georgians, 3–4 million; Tadzhiks, 2 million; Turkmens and Kirghiz, 1½ million. Most other non-European peoples under one million: there are 50 recognised nationalities in the Caucasus.

The non-Russian peoples were detached from their homelands by two main activities. Some peoples, especially the Tartars, were forcibly removed from their ancestral lands and were resettled in Central Asia. Those who remain undisturbed have had to accommodate a vast regulated immigration of Russians into their lands for the great Soviet programmes of agricultural development. Russian and Soviet internal imperialism has not been marked by the expropriation and extermination of 'frontier' peoples, as in North America (except in a brief period after the Revolution), nor have the frontier peoples been assigned a second-class status, like the Negro in the United States: but the culture shock of Russian and Soviet assimilation of ancient Islamic societies has been even more complete than in North America.

Thus during the first four decades of the twentieth century the white dominance established during the nineteenth century was reinforced and preserved. Of course there were clear indications of massive changes in the balance of power within the white-dominated world. Sea power, which had shifted from the Mediterranean to the Atlantic – and to the Pacific – gave way to land power: the mighty land-based states, the U.S.S.R. and the U.S.A., took over as world leaders from Britain, France and Germany. But apart from the challenge hurled down by Japan, the non-white peoples remained spectators of world events. Their attempts to create their own international organisation appeared puny.

A Pan-African Congress was held in London in 1900 and was attended by delegates from the Caribbean, the United States and Britain. The Congress left hardly any mark, and not until 1919 was the event repeated, in Paris. The second Congress is remembered for the leadership of W. E. B. Du Bois (1868–1963) the American black sociologist and publicist, who articulated the theme of race conflict and the black challenge to white dominance. Thanks largely to his endeavours, three more Pan-African Congresses were held in the next eight years. Thereafter Du Bois moved towards communism and after visits to the Soviet Union he settled in Africa, where he died. He did not attend the fifth Congress held at Manchester in 1945 where, without acclaim, several of the future leaders of Africa (including Nkrumah and Kenyatta) heralded the resurgence of colonised black peoples. What linked all these gatherings was the conviction that the subjugation of black people in the United States and other metropolitan countries was an aspect of the white colonialism which also held down almost the whole of Africa. Imperialism, they were saying, was indivisible.

A similar contribution was made by the International Congress Against Colonial Oppression and Imperialism held at Brussels in 1927. The Congress included representatives of the European Left (Henri Barbusse, George Lansbury, Fenner Brockway, Ernst Toller) and a large number of delegates from China, Africa, Latin America, and other colonial or neo-colonial territories. Among these, the best known were Mohammad Hatta of Indonesia and Jawaharlal Nehru of India. The main target was 'British capitalist brigandage', and the main ally was perceived as the Soviet Union. The Congress set up a permanent body, the League Against Imperialism, which some hoped would become a non-white counter-force to the League of Nations.

However pungent the appeal made by such efforts and however dynamic their leading personalities, they were insufficient to challenge white dominance. This was to come mainly because of the impact of a phenomenon peculiar to the twentieth century: the phenomenon of world war.

3 The Melting-Pot of War

THERE have been few years during the twentieth century in which a major war was not being waged, but the machinery of destruction reached its zenith in the Second World War and in the war in Vietnam. These were the cauldrons in which the structure of white dominance was melted and broken. The wars which came before were a prelude, though themselves contributing to the transformation.

For Alfred Zimmern, as a young lecturer at Oxford, the defeat of Russia by Japan in 1905 was the watershed. He told his class that he was putting aside Greek history that morning: 'Because, I said, I feel I must speak to you about the most important historical event which has happened, or is likely to happen, in our lifetime; the victory of a non-white people over a white people.'[1] Many others, especially in the colonised lands of Asia, saw in the victories of Tsushima and Mukden an equal significance. Yet Japan was really imitating the West in its path of conquest and dominance. Japan's victories led to the further sub-jugation of Asian peoples in Taiwan, Korea and Manchuria.

The First World War involved hundreds of thousands of men from Asia and Africa in the fighting and in support of the armies as workers behind the battle-lines. Indian soldiers fought alongside British troops in France, and beside men from Australia in Gallipoli. French African troops fought in all the great battles, and contributed to the shambles of Verdun. A Labour Corps was recruited in China to work behind the trenches, and among the clerks who accompanied them was an observant young Chinese, Chou En-lai. Even more casually, a Vietnamese cook on a merchant ship found himself in wartime Britain and France: the future Ho Chi Minh. Yet although so many from Asia and Africa were sucked into the jaws of war, the first impact was limited to that of personal experience: black and brown men discovered that on the battlefield they were equal with white men in misery and death, and in survival. The experience produced no immediately discernible political consequences. They did not realise that the First World War had drained the life-force out of the European empires.[2]

The revolution in Russia made a greater impact, for it was Lenin's thesis that Asia and Africa formed the 'reserves' of the world revolution. Lenin emphasised that by forming 'armies composed of subject peoples' the imperial powers were exposing themselves to possible resistance by their subjects. The (Third) Communist International was founded in 1919 to create the conditions for international communism. The Comintern declared: 'Imperialism is therefore capitalism moribund and decaying. It is the final stage of development of the capitalist system. It is the threshold of world social revolution.'

However, the immediate effects were limited. Communist attempts to organise revolution in India were largely in the hands of M. N. Roy, an important ideologue but not a successful organiser. The British authorities remorselessly suppressed the Indian Communists in the 1920s, and the party was a spent force for twenty years. The second great offensive was in China, and the efforts of the Kuomintang (K.M.T.) to oppose foreign imperialism (especially the creeping Japanese aggression) were reinforced by the supply of Russian military experts to the Whampoa Military Academy where most of the new Chinese leaders were trained. But the main beneficiary was Chiang Kai-shek who used his Russian-trained generals to wipe out Mao Tse-tung's rural guerrillas. In both China and India the Russians guessed wrong. (Concerning Gandhi, the Comintern pronounced: 'Gandhism is more and more becoming an ideology directed against mass revolution. It must be strongly combated by Communism.' Not until ten years after independence was Gandhi 'rehabilitated' in Soviet ideology.)

The effects of the rise of the Soviet Union were indirect. The Comintern pronounced in 1928 that their task was to ensure 'The recognition of the rights of all nations, irrespective of race, to complete self-determination. . . . Wide and determined struggle against the imposition of any kind of limitation and restriction upon any nationality, nation or race. Complete equality for all nations and races.' This was a clear call to rising leaders such as Jawaharlal Nehru or Johnson Kenyatta.

As wars continued in the era 'between the wars', 1918–39, the dissembling attitude of Britain, France and the United States in the face of aggression seemed to confirm the Leninist thesis that imperialism represented the last, degenerate stage of the capitalist order. Chinese resistance to Japanese invasion seemed to evoke no response from the West; it was left to the U.S.S.R. to furnish aid, and to Indian and other colonised peoples to offer symbolic support. The invasion of Ethiopia by Italy aroused even greater fury. The repulse of the Italian forces at Adowa in 1896 was reckoned as one of the few victories of black or brown men over white invaders. (The repulse of the French by the Chinese at Langson on the northern frontier of Vietnam in 1884 was another symbolic defeat of whites by non-whites which provided an ominous foretaste of things to come.) The conquest of Ethiopia by Mussolini's armies in 1935 – while the world found excuses for doing nothing – appeared to be a complete demonstration of how much stronger white solidarity was than Western protestations of democratic belief in freedom and justice (see Map 1). An upswell of black solidarity arose in reply, and black men in the United States, the Caribbean and in British colonies in Africa, who had no effective means of communicating with each other, made their spontaneous gestures of protest in a manner which almost anticipated the mobilising of Black Power movements.

Ethiopia was soon forgotten by the Western world. Haile Selassie was booed by Italian onlookers at Geneva, and the white world turned to other problems nearer at hand: for Britain and France the real issue dominating the later 1930s was the goal of Adolf Hitler.

The racist element in Nazism was less important to the Western democracies than the threat of territorial expansion, for they too accepted many of Adolf Hitler's assumptions about racial difference. Denis Brogan writes: 'It would be highly unrealistic not to note the fact that in the years between the wars the United States was only outdistanced by Germany as a market for race theories, some of them crude enough to have suited Hitler'.[3] From the start, Hitler made it quite clear that his was a mission to establish a domain of racial difference. The Nazis preached the 'leadership principle' which laid down that all Germans must follow Hitler in enforcing the supremacy of the Nordic race over 'lower races' like the Latin and Slav and over 'subhuman races' like the Jews and Negroes.[4] It was paradoxical that Hitler should draw Mussolini's Italy into his orbit, for the doctrine of Nordic, Aryan supremacy overrode the Fascist pronunciamento that it was Italy's destiny to rule the Mediterranean as heir to Rome. It was part of the Nazi view of world history that decadent Rome had fallen to the 'pure' Aryan invaders from the north. Italian fascism was racist in its treatment of non-Europeans, but not in regard to Jews.

Methodically, the Nazis eliminated all Jewish elements from the national life. The books of Jewish writers were burned, and all Jews were removed from positions in public life and education. The shock to the German Jews was traumatic, for they were amongst the most 'assimilated' of all their communities; their life-style was indistinguishable from that of other Germans. When Hitler decided to hunt out all the Jews, it was necessary to identify them by pinning the Star of David to their shops and business premises and also to their persons, for they could not be distinguished by appearance, speech or name. The movement of Jewish refugees from Germany to Britain, the United States and other countries was one of the few Jewish emigrations which have aroused no anti-Semitic protests. In part the reason was the sympathetic attitude of all those opposed to Nazism, but perhaps more important the emigrants were almost all middle class, professional people, including a number of distinguished intellectuals.

When war began in September 1939 it was to be very much a war about race; though this was disguised from almost all the opponents of Hitler, who regarded the struggle as a war for freedom. The two main statements upon the ideals for which the Anglo-American alliance (later called the United Nations) were fighting to defeat Germany – together with Japan – were those issued in 1941 by Roosevelt and Churchill. In January 1941, President Roosevelt in his address to Congress identified 'four essential human freedoms': freedom of speech, freedom of worship, freedom from want, and freedom from fear. The 'Four Freedoms' clearly did not envisage freedom from racial discrimination or persecution as a basic necessity: probably because for Roosevelt race and racism was only a tiresome feature of domestic southern politics. Eight months later the 'Atlantic Charter' was issued, following a meeting between Roosevelt and Churchill aboard a British battleship. The eight points therein promulgated were more concrete than the Four Freedoms, but they also failed to identify race as a salient factor, for the statement that 'all the men in all the lands may live out their lives in freedom from fear and want' was merely a recapitulation of Roosevelt's message to Congress: and that was the nearest approach the Allies made to the question of racial equality. Churchill took an early opportunity to make it clear that the third point promising 'the right of all peoples to choose the form of government under which they will live' did not mean that the British intended to withdraw from India.

For Hitler, the war on the eastern front gave the opportunity to apply the principles of a superior race ruling over lesser races. His aim was to clear out most of the indigenous peoples and plant German colonies in the eastern lands. The Poles and Ukrainians were treated as *Un-*

termenschen, lower races, and were mobilised as slave labour on farms and in factories managed by Germans. The Jews and the gypsies were not even *Untermenschen*; for them, the Ultimate Solution, death — genocide — in the gas chamber. The Nazi ideology was transmitted to their allies: the Romanian Iron Guard and the Croatian Fascists applied the Ultimate Solution to their own Jewish communities, and also to the Serbs who were classified as sub-humans. Nazi ideology ran into difficulties in occupied Denmark and Norway, for here the Nordic race was found in its purest form. When Danes and Norwegians resisted the German occupation by non-violent but often effective protest (as when the King of Denmark threatened to cut down the swastika if it were hoisted over the royal palace: so that it wasn't) the Nazis felt unable to apply the methods of repression which were imposed without hesitation upon Poles or Serbs.

Similarly, the Germans waged war upon their enemies according to two completely different codes. In fighting the British, and later the Americans, the Germans stayed fairly closely to the Geneva Convention: indeed, the battle of the *Luftwaffe* against the Royal Air Force was conducted almost in terms of medieval chivalry, especially to the fallen foe. The war against the Russians, and against the different resistance movements, was devoid of any feeling for the enemy, who must be exterminated. Perhaps not surprisingly, the Russians retaliated in the same terms.

If, in the West, the Second World War was a kind of civil war between peoples who had become estranged but who must eventually be reunited (and Allied propaganda emphasised that the war was against the Nazis, not against Germany), the war in Asia was much more openly a race war. The Japanese betrayal — the decision to resign from the Anglo-American club in East Asia and lead a war of brown men against white men — opened up a gulf between Japan and the West which, it seemed, nothing could ever bridge again. Japan announced that the day of the white man in Asia was finished; the Greater East Asia Co-Prosperity Sphere was to be the first international community in which brown men, together, would demonstrate their superiority over the whites. The British — and very much more, the Americans — retaliated with an outburst of hatred which consigned the Japanese to the category of sub-humans.

The Japanese victory in South-east Asia in the early months of 1942 was beyond their wildest hopes. The British were pushed back to the borders of India; the Americans were forced back across the Pacific almost to their naval base at Pearl Harbour, and in their retreat unprecedented numbers of Allied troops became prisoners. The capitulation of the British forces in Malaya at Singapore, in February 1942, was the most disastrous event in British military history; 100,000 British, Australian and Indian soldiers surrendered to a Japanese commander whose own forces were numerically much smaller. Not surprisingly, the Japanese treated these prisoners – and also the Dutch in Indonesia who put up even less of a struggle – as men who had failed to uphold their military honour. The European prisoners were put to humiliating menial labour; the most notorious being the construction of the Death Railway which was built to link Burma and Thailand. The Indian prisoners were wooed as potential recruits for the Japanese.

The build-up of a Japanese-sponsored 'Indian National Army' (I.N.A.) was given an enormous boost by the leadership of Subhas Chandra Bose, *Netaji*, or Great General, to his followers.[5] Bose had been under arrest in India in the early months of the war, but he escaped to Afghanistan and from there made his way to Germany. He embraced the whole Nazi philosophy, including the concept of Aryan supremacy which he applied to India to prove that the Indo-Aryans were superior to the *Mlecchas*, the unclean invaders from England. Bose raised an Indian legion in Germany, but after Japan's triumphant conquest of South-east Asia he made an adventurous journey by German submarine to Indonesia. He became the head of the *Azad Hind* (Free India) government and urged the Japanese to commit the I.N.A. to fight against the British defending the borderland between Burma and India.

News of the Japanese conquest filtered back to Britain and America. Americans were infuriated by the 'betrayal' with which Japan had started the war: the surprise attack upon Pearl Harbour. When news arrived of the hardships endured by American prisoners taken at Bataan in the Philippines and subjected to a 'death march' American fury boiled over. They were able to exact revenge upon those Japanese within their grasp: the 112,000 people of Japanese origin – over 71,000 of whom were American citizens – living mainly in the coastal-land of California and Washington State. Immediately after Pearl Harbour the cry arose that this was a fifth column, planted to spy and sabotage the American war effort. Earl Warren, a leading Republican politician (elected Governor of California in November 1942, and later appointed Chief Justice of the United States Supreme Court) called for the expulsion and internment of all persons of Japanese origin. The military commander on the West Coast, General De Witt, underlined the demand with the observation 'It makes no difference whether the Jap is a citizen or not. He's still a Jap.'[6] Despite his concern for the Four Freedoms, President Roosevelt signed the order for their deportation on 19 February 1942. The order was directed against all persons of enemy origin, but immediately the military command announced that the 80,000 residents on the west coast who had come from Germany and Italy would be exempted. Every Japanese-American was rounded up and removed into the interior to be imprisoned in concentration camps, behind barbed wire and under military guard. Ironically, many of the camps were located in the Indian reservations because of the outcry from citizens of other areas who feared they might have to accept the Japanese.

Many of those who called for repressive measures against the Japanese internees were from the South: they had no personal experience of Asians but were bitterly racist because of their attitude to blacks and Jews. Representative John Rankin of Mississippi called for all blood donated to hospitals by blacks and Japanese to be separately labelled so as not to 'contaminate' the veins of Caucasians. The few Americans who opposed internment of the Japanese belonged to radical or left-wing groups. Norman Thomas, who stood several times as Socialist candidate for the American presidency, was virtually the only national leader to speak out. The National Association for the Advancement of Colored People (N.A.A.C.P.) did not miss the overall racist significance of internment. The N.A.A.C.P. announced: 'If Asiatic-Americans can be reduced to bondage, deprived of citizenship and of property, the same thing can be done to Afro-Americans and Jews.'[7]

Neighbouring Canada adopted a similar policy. Canadian troops had helped defend Hong Kong, and stories of Japanese atrocities followed its capitulation. The Canadian-Japanese community in British Columbia, about 22,000 in number, were also deported from the coastal region and interned. The British Columbia politician, Ian Mackenzie, demanded that after the war they be expelled from Canada to Japan.[8]

In wartime propaganda, emanating from Hollywood and other film studios, the Japanese were invariably portrayed as sub-human monsters. A wartime 'Japanese type' was evolved, more ape than man, with huge, hideous teeth, low forehead and shambling gait. In the scenes of brutality in such films as *Betrayal from the East* and *Black Dragon*, the Japanese-Americans, the *Nisei*, were depicted as traitors and spies.

When wartime propaganda films handled German themes these almost always emphasised that it was the Nazis who were the enemy; such films took care to include at least one 'good German' to indicate that the war in the West was not directed against a whole nation. There were no 'good Japanese' in the films about the Pacific war.

President Roosevelt spent quite a lot of his time thinking about the kind of world which would arise out of the Second World War. He was determined that European colonialism should be ended: the nations of Asia (though not of Africa) must be free to embrace the democratic ideal. And so he planned with his advisers how to get the British out of Hong Kong and the French out of Indo-China. In addition, he and his advisers were planning for the democratisation of militarist Japan when the war ended. This process could not be left to the Japanese themselves, and so an American superstructure would be erected to carry out democratisation. Maybe it would be necessary to introduce a new breed of man to replace the stubborn Japanese? The British Minister in Washington spent a weekend with the President and reported that (as one account puts it) Roosevelt had been 'burbling away . . . on the possibility of bringing about a cross-breeding of European and various Asian races in the Far East in order to produce a stock less delinquent than the Japanese'.[9]

The same solution to the inadequacy of the brown peoples – cross-breeding with those of the superior race – occurred independently to Leopold Amery, the British Cabinet Minister in charge of India. Ruminating over the possibility of independence for India in future, he suggested to the Viceroy:

If India is to be really capable of holding its own in future without direct British control from outside I am not sure that it will not need an increasing infusion of stronger Nordic blood, whether by settlement or intermarriage or otherwise. Possibly it has been a real mistake of ours in the past not to encourage Indian princes to marry English wives . . . and so breed a more virile type of native ruler. Perhaps all that may yet come about.[10]

It is not easy to discover how these racial ideas, enunciated by Roosevelt and Amery, differed essentially from Hitler's ideology of a master race in Europe.

As America mobilised for war, military conscription was introduced on a massive scale. When black Americans were called to arms they were drafted to separate black units, as had been the invariable custom since the Civil War of the 1860s. Most Negroes were drafted into the army and were put into the transport, the stores and other 'rear echelon' units. There were Negro combatant units, and these were organised into all-black brigades and divisions. Although after the United States found itself at war with Japan, all the *Nisei* who were in the armed forces were discharged, a few of them were permitted to get out of their camps by volunteering for an all-*Nisei* fighting unit. In the Pacific war American intelligence needed personnel knowing Japanese, and *Nisei* were recruited for intelligence work. No *Nisei* combatants were sent to the Pacific theatre of war. Similarly, there were no black and brown fighting men in Normandy and the invasion from the West: they were sent to Italy, where it was assumed by the American general staff that conditions were not so tough.

Some black non-combatant units spent a period of time in Britain before D-Day, and this posed a delicate problem in Anglo-American relations. The British attitude to race was still based upon the theory that in Britain everyone was treated equally, regardless of colour. The American approach (strongly influenced by the high proportion of southerners who graduated from West Point) was that black troops must be segregated from white. If black and white American soldiers collided in British pubs or dance halls there was trouble. The American army tried to persuade the British authorities to designate certain places of entertainment exclusively for the Negroes and to exclude them from other places; the British somewhat sanctimoniously declined to co-operate. However, the white and black American soldiers made their own arrangements for going their separate ways.

Questions of race and colour were salient in other countries of the United Nations, fighting for democracy and the rights of free peoples. South Africa joined Britain in the war against Germany by a very narrow margin of choice; a substantial proportion of the Afrikaners were strongly sympathetic to Hitler, and had their own quasi-Nazi organisation, the *Ossewa Brandwag*. Under the leadership of Smuts, British South Africans – and a proportion of the Afrikaners, especially of the Cape – participated actively in the war effort. South African forces served in the North African campaigns, and later in Italy. The fighting men were all white; black Africans, and also Indians, were recruited, but only for transport, engineer, and other services in which the soldiers did not carry arms. When these black and brown South Africans found themselves in the Western Desert alongside soldiers from India operating infantry weapons, artillery and armour they were humiliated. For South Africa, the comradeship of arms was confined to the white race. When ships carrying Indian troops docked at South African ports, the Indian officers stayed on board; to disembark was to invite exclusion from hotels and clubs.

The war progressed with scarcely any recognition by American or British leaders that these things existed. Nor did they realise that among the civilian population the war was having a massive effect upon non-white people. In the United States, the major war industries were located in the North and the Midwest and on the Pacific coast. It was in these areas that the mass production of tanks and planes and ships was concentrated. Industry needed labour, and was ready to pay good wages. Under these conditions, skin-colour was not the main consideration. Out of the rural South, Negro workers in thousands moved to Detroit, to Los Angeles, and to all the other centres where the weapons of war were being built. They migrated never to return. On a much smaller scale, the British war industry – mainly reliant upon a massive mobilisation of British women – turned to sources overseas. From the Caribbean and from India there arrived technicians to work in British factories; the 'Bevin boys' as they were called. To these black and brown newcomers, Britain – even in wartime – seemed a good place to live in.

There was a reverse process: the exposure of many thousands of British and American service personnel to the experience of Asia and the Middle East. Previously, the small numbers of professional British soldiers and American marines in India and China had lived largely self-contained lives in cantonments, forts, and other restricted areas. They had developed a certain contemptuous familiarity with Asian ways, and the vocabulary of British regular soldiers was much interlarded with Hindustani terms, while the speech of American marines and sailors had a Chinese flavour. The encounter between East and West, in so far as it took place, reinforced the Western sense of innate superiority.

When British and American conscripts were decanted in the unfamiliar East they were more vulnerable to the environment. They took over the outlook of racial superiority of the professional soldiers, and their vocabulary was augmented to include such all-embracing terms as *Wog, Gippy, Gook, Sambo* (they actually addressed all Asians as Joe). However, they lacked the panache of the old professionals; they were bewildered, bored, rather pathetic, and far from home. They got drunk disgustingly; they lusted after the local women without discrimination; they drifted about on leave looking woebegone and bedraggled. In the case of the British they had too little pay, and so tried to beat down a shopkeeper or a bartender; in the case of the Americans they had too much pay, and they earned contempt from the bell boys and call girls to whom they handed out dollars when the local price was in cents.

The British conscripts, most of them good Labour voters, were just as imperialistic in their attitude to the 'lesser breeds' as any Poona colonel of fiction; the Americans took with them their innate sense of superiority to black and also brown peoples. The effect of this temporary exposure of millions of Anglo-Americans to unknown cultures has been portrayed with cautious sentimentality in *South Pacific* and more crudely in the novel *Virgin Soldiers* by Leslie Thomas. Racist attitudes, previously latent, were now active; and they did not become dormant with the coming of peace. When conscripts went home, the Arabs and Indians and Chinese remembered that they were not supermen after all.

The effects of the Second World War were least obvious in Africa. Apart from the restoration of Haile Selassie to his throne, there were no moves towards African self-government. Indeed, the African territories under British rule now attained their widest extent (see Map 1, page 136). It was in Asia, and particularly in South-east Asia, that the decline and fall of Western colonialism was made inevitable by the wartime experience.

From 1942 until 1944, the Japanese Greater East Asia Co-Prosperity Sphere appeared to have established a permanent Pan-Asian order over a region larger than Europe or North America. In their treatment of their Asian vassals the Japanese often did not bother to disguise their dominant status. A Japanese sergeant would administer a face-slapping to a Burmese or Indonesian without hesitation. At higher levels, there was not much effort to disguise the puppet status of those South-east Asians installed in authority: 'One had to recognise the "Made in Japan" stamp on one's forehead' observed U Nu who was designated as the Foreign Minister of Burma.[11] And yet South-east Asians who would have risen no higher than schoolmasters or customs inspectors or sergeants under the Europeans now found themselves ministers, generals, judges. Burma, the Philippines, and eventually the former Dutch East Indies — now Indonesia — were declared to be independent nations, allies, not subordinates of the Japanese. The top leaders — Subhas Chandra Bose, Dr Ba Maw of Burma, José P. Laurel of the Philippines and Sukarno of Indonesia — were invited to participate in spectacular war conferences at Tokyo. More important, young South-east Asians were trained to lead armies. The Burmese 'Thirty

Comrades', led by *Bogyoke* (Great Captain) Aung San, formed the leadership for a Burma National Army; and similar forces were raised in Indonesia and the Philippines. These military forces provided the strongest guarantee that the independence conceded by Japan could not easily be snatched away.

Not all the peoples of South-east Asia shone in the glory of the Rising Sun. In Malaya and Singapore the Chinese community – over one-third of the total population – were treated from the start as the enemies of Japan. Many young Chinese took to the jungle, where they were supplied by the 'Home Army', the Chinese of the villages and towns. The jungle guerrillas – the Malayan People's Anti-Japanese Army (M.P.A.J.A.) – were led by Chinese Communists, formerly active in trade unions. Their activities were confined to sabotage and ambush, but they established a firm reputation among the Malayan Chinese as resistance heroes.

Similarly, in Indo-China – that is, in the territories which later became Vietnam – an anti-Japanese resistance movement was organised by Ho Chi Minh under the name of Viet Minh. Although receiving sparse military aid from China, and later from American sources, the Viet Minh was essentially a national movement opposed to the domination of all foreigners.

Japan's empire suddenly crumbled under the weight of the Allied attacks from 1944 onwards. On the Burma front, Bose's dream of an I.N.A. victory and a March on Delhi dissolved into the reality of the I.N.A.'s defeat, along with their Japanese overlords, and the re-occupation of Burma by British-Indian forces. Dr Ba Maw was jailed as a Japanese collaborator, but Aung San and the Thirty Comrades were more skilful in switching sides at the correctly judged moment. Their Burma Army disappeared into the jungle, and re-emerged as the Anti-Fascist People's Freedom League (A.F.P.F.L.). Although some British military administrators found this *bouleversement* hard to take, the Supreme Commander, Admiral Mountbatten, decided to accept Aung San's proffered support. His army was supposed to be disbanded, with some units being enlisted into the British forces while the others were demobilised. However, with great skill, Aung San succeeded in keeping former units together under their old officers, notably the Thirty Comrades, while those demobilised were formed into what was presented as an old comrades' association, the People's Volunteer Organisation (P.V.O.). In reality the P.V.O. remained an organised, uniformed military force, available to Aung San in a national struggle.

The British government had planned to put post-war Burma into a kind of political deep-freeze, but thanks to Aung San's determined leadership independence could not be postponed into the future. Britain had been accustomed to rely upon Indian battalions to keep order in Burma when required; but now India was demanding its own independence, Indian soldiers could no longer be employed as British mercenaries. Under the threat of a general strike and a possible armed rising, Aung San got all he wanted. Independence was won in January 1948; but by then Aung San was dead — shot by an assassin.[12] South-east Asia was to undergo a long and terrible experience of the truth of the prophecy that 'they that take the sword shall perish with the sword'. And so, though Burma was reoccupied by the former imperial power, this was temporary. The Philippines were reoccupied by American forces, though only after the path had been blasted by bombing, leaving the old city of Manila a smoking ruin. The rest of South-east Asia still remained under over-all Japanese control when, on 6 August 1945, the American atomic bomb was dropped on Hiroshima and 100,000 people died. Three days later a second atomic bomb was dropped, and the Emperor of Japan capitulated.

The technical development of the vast 'Manhattan Project' reached the critical point where a bomb could be exploded from the air only after the defeat of Germany in Europe. Nevertheless, Asians have not ceased to speculate whether an American President would have dared to order an atomic attack upon a German city. It remains a grim fact that the only nuclear attack ever made was performed by white men against brown men. The poison from that decision will suppurate until the twentieth century is finished.

Because of the sudden and unexpected capitulation of Japan, most of the countries of South-east Asia went through an interlude in which one master had stood down and no other had arrived. In Malaya, the guerrillas of the M.P.A.J.A. heard of the news of Hiroshima and emerged from the jungle expecting to meet representatives of the Chinese army. They were amazed when British forces under Mountbatten landed at Penang and Singapore and proceeded to take over the administration. In a daze, the jungle guerrillas handed over most of their arms and permitted themselves to be demobilised. It was another three years before they made their bid for power again. However, in the brief moment between the fall of the Japanese and the arrival of the British, the Chinese jungle fighters exacted vengeance upon those who had collaborated with the Rising Sun: most of the collaborators were

Malays, and the Malay population did not forget that moment when the Chinese exercised their mastery over Malaya.

The reassertion of the Western presence was much less easy in Indo-China and Indonesia. The task of occupation was suddenly and unexpectedly switched from the American forces under General MacArthur to the British-Indian forces under Admiral Mountbatten. Mountbatten was one of the few Anglo-American commanders sensitive to the reality that the old pre-1939 world had departed forever. He was only prepared to use his forces in the limited role of disarming the Japanese and rescuing Allied prisoners of war; he was not going to commit them to the attempt to renew Western colonial domination. He had the responsibility of taking over Indo-China and Indonesia. He approached the task cautiously.

Neither France nor the Netherlands wanted the British to settle into the occupation of their territories: perhaps they might decide to stay permanently! These two countries, staggering out of five years of Nazi occupation, tried to rush their own forces to South-east Asia. By the time they arrived, they found that Mountbatten's representatives had gone a long way to recognising the legitimacy of Ho Chi Minh in Vietnam and Sukarno in Indonesia. Hastily taking over from the British, the French and the Dutch tried to reassert the colonial overlordship they had so ignominiously surrendered to the Japanese.[13]

For four years the tenacious Dutch tried to bring Indonesia back into their orbit. Their forces were opposed by the Indonesian army created by the Japanese and, despite limited successes, the Netherlands could not substitute for the Sukarno government a regime of their own which was acceptable. Dutch military operations depended heavily upon a reconstituted colonial army, whose soldiers were drawn largely from the island of Ambon or Amboyna in the South Moluccas. The Ambonese belonged to the Melanesian, not the Malay race. Ambon had been Dutch for over three hundred years, and its inhabitants were all pious Calvinists, strongly responsive to Dutch influence and with no feeling of identity with the Muslims of Java and western Indonesia.

The Dutch campaign led to the first counter-action by Asians, expressing solidarity in the fight against imperialism. Led by India, the new states of Asia, together with some in the Middle East, imposed a ban upon all Dutch aircraft from landing at Asian airfields. The ban made it difficult for the Netherlands to reinforce their position in Indonesia. At length, when Australian trade unions had also joined in a boycott of Dutch ships, the Netherlands government decided to recognise the independence of Indonesia, and in 1949 a formal agreement was signed and the Dutch withdrew from their former empire in the Indies, retaining control of New Guinea for a limited period.

At the same time, the Ambonese proclaimed their own separate independence as the Republic of the South Moluccas. They were unable to resist Indonesian pressure, and the little republic was ruthlessly repressed. Feeling a responsibility to their colonial soldiers, the Dutch government evacuated many Ambonese troops, together with their families, to the Netherlands. The move was expected to be only temporary until a *modus vivendi* could be arranged with Indonesia. Still demanding their own independence, the Ambonese remained in the Netherlands, and by the 1970s there was no possibility of their return. However, they declined to integrate into Dutch society, formed their own government in exile, and lived apart in their own camps; yet another group of refugees who could not go home. The young Dutch-born Ambonese remain as strongly attached to the island they have never seen as their elders. When a Dutch train was hijacked by the Ambonese in 1975, the urban guerrillas involved were all young men.

The realistic Dutch turned their backs upon their old empire and proceeded to create a new prosperity within the emerging European community. France was less prepared to forget the glories of empire. It was necessary to accept the independence of Syria and the Lebanon, but in north and west Africa, in the Caribbean, and in Indo-China a great French empire remained intact: or so it seemed. Very soon it became clear that the main challenge would come from Vietnam. The rest of Indo-China — Laos and Cambodia — could be restored to the former, traditional order of things, but Ho Chi Minh was not prepared for any compromise which denied the reality of independence. More and more French troops were ordered to Vietnam; almost the whole of the Foreign Legion (a high proportion of whom were former Nazis) and colonial troops from Morocco, Algeria and Senegal. Although all the advantages seemed to be with the French command they were gradually compelled to abandon their frontier posts, and then many of their positions in the rural areas. The forces of Ho Chi Minh, led by General Giap, were transformed from jungle guerrillas into well-trained operational troops. This transformation was observed with growing alarm by the United States.

It will be recalled that the American Office of Strategic Services (O.S.S.: the forerunner of the C.I.A.) had actively assisted Ho Chi

Minh in organising his guerrillas. However, American policy towards 'liberation movements' was undergoing a total about-turn, in consequence of events in China. China had been a major field for American economic exploitation since the nineteenth century. It had also been *the* major field for American idealism. American protestant missionaries had gone to China in thousands, and hundreds of young Chinese had been sent to the United States for higher education. There were even American universities, such as 'Yale in China' which were transplants of American culture in the Far East.

Americans had been subjected to a remarkable propaganda exercise by the 'China Lobby' in the United States Congress which succeeded in convincing Americans that the struggle waged by the forces of Generalissimo Chiang Kai-shek against Japan was much more formidable than the dismal reality of retreats and covert understandings with the Japanese which the K.M.T. leaders conducted while they accumulated their private fortunes. Madame Chiang, a member of a Methodist family, projected a most effective image of 'Christian China' standing up to heathen Japan. It was assumed that because China was a republic, with a president, it was really remarkably like America.*

When the K.M.T. forces ignominiously collapsed in the face of Mao Tse-tung's Red Army, and the whole of China rapidly became the People's Republic, the shock was traumatic. Nothing like this had ever happened before. The United States myth was that they won all the wars. Yet despite massive American military aid to Chiang Kai-shek, and the attachment of senior American military advisers to his staff, this war was decisively lost and the rump of the K.M.T. forces were evacuated to Taiwan by the American navy. Thus it had to be acknowledged that the United States had 'lost' China to communism. No American leader was prepared to ask the question as to exactly how, or in what sense, the United States had a China to lose.[14] Once again, a nation which had been admitted to honorary membership of the white club (at any rate by American humanitarians and idealists) had resigned from the club. American ideas underwent galvanic changes. Defeated Japan, subjected to all kinds of humiliation,

---

* Geoffrey Gorer, *The Americans* (London, 1948) somewhat accentuates American cultural tendencies in his very lively analysis, yet his chapter 'Lesser Breeds' is shrewd in regard to the American tendency to equate any country that has a monarchy with England under George III, and any republican country with the America of Washington and Andrew Jackson: 'The Chinese have been the special recipients of this form of flattery' he wrote (p. 174) when the tendency was at its height in the United States.

suddenly became an important bastion of the United States, and began that return to esteem which, by the 1970s, has re-established that country in American eyes as perhaps the finest example of the Protestant work ethic.

Meanwhile, there was Vietnam, visibly failing to stand up to communism. When the French government approached America for arms, planes and other equipment, they found willing listeners. Along with American military hardware, American observers began to arrive in Saigon. They were not impressed by what they saw. The French colonial regime was paramount, and the attempt to rehabilitate the puppet Emperor, Bao Dai, failed to evoke any Vietnamese response. The implication of any American intervention was that they must take over responsibilities from the French; there could be no handover to Vietnamese leaders, as yet. Almost imperceptibly, the Americans began to ease aside the French.

The process was accelerated by two main factors. In 1953, John Foster Dulles became Secretary of State, and under the easygoing presidency of Eisenhower assumed virtual control of foreign policy. He adopted the policy of 'brinkmanship', of escalating military pressure almost but not quite to the point of outright war. He carried the conception of foreign policy as morality to a similar extreme. For him, South-east Asia was a set of dominoes, standing upright in file; if one domino should fall, all would fall. Hence, Vietnam was vital, as the outstanding tottering domino.

The Vietnamese domino almost toppled over when the French high command committed its forces to the defence of a remote outpost, Dien Bien Phu. From March until May 1954, Dien Bien Phu withstood attack after attack. Reinforcements and ammunition were parachuted in, for the French command believed that the Viet Minh would destroy themselves in their attempt to take the place. They had fatally underestimated the determination of their opponents, who enjoyed artillery superiority and pounded the defenders under the ground. At last, a human assault wave roared over the defence, and Dien Bien Phu's 16,000 defenders surrendered.

John Foster Dulles offered to provide the French with two nuclear weapons in order to retaliate, but France had had enough. Premier Mendès-France undertook to secure a settlement, and by July 1954 a truce was negotiated at Geneva whereby France withdrew from all Vietnam north of the 17th parallel of latitude. The Geneva agreement was virtually the end of the French presence in Vietnam. Most of the

French military transports bore the dejected legionaries and colonial troops to Algeria. Among those who had fought for the French in Vietnam was the Algerian sergeant, Ahmed Ben Bella. On 1 November 1954, a revolt broke out in the Aures Mountains of Algeria; among the resistance leaders was ex-sergeant Ben Bella.

However, the eyes of the world were more and more fixed upon Vietnam. When the French withdrew, the Americans planned to 'Vietnamese' the fight against the Communists and their attention turned to a pious Catholic functionary, Ngo Dinh Diem, then a recluse in the United States with the Maryknoll Fathers. In July 1954 he replaced Bao Dai as head of state – President Diem. He soon gave evidence of all the necessary determination and ruthlessness, but he did not satisfy the American dream of 'democratising' South Vietnam. Although he despised and rejected the French, his political philosophy, Personalism, was a form of the French cult of Existentialism. Looking around for a solution, Diem turned for advice to British officers who had helped to end the Communist 'Emergency' in Malaya.

The anti-insurgent campaign in Malaya was the one success-story for 'the free world' in the 1950s in Asia. The British had succeeded in containing the revolt which was launched in 1948 by former M.P.A.J.A. fighters. They isolated the jungle Communists, first by persuading the Malays that this was a purely Chinese affair, and then by successfully changing the image of the guerrillas into that of *terrorists*, bandits, enemies of the people. And finally they picked off the Communist leaders, one by one. Napoleon said the British were a nation of shopkeepers; he might equally have called the Chinese a nation of shopkeepers. Now, in Malaya, the British went shopping. They put a price on the head of every Communist leader. If it was not enough to buy him, they raised the price. Sooner or later one of his followers brought in the head for identification, and hastily departed to set up a filling station or a hotel on the other side of Malaya. By 1960, the Emergency was officially ended.

So President Diem tried to benefit from British advice. One of his ideas was to found *agrovilles*, strategic hamlets, which had been a part of the success in isolating the Communists in Malaya. The American advisers were not pleased by this adoption of seemingly unaggressive, un-American methods.

Dulles remained Secretary of State until 1959. With his departure, the momentum of American intervention slowed down. It was very worrying that despite a large counter-revolutionary programme to win the 'hearts and minds' of the Vietnamese peasants, the countryside remained largely under the grip of the Communist guerrillas, to whom the name of Viet Cong was now attached. What should be done? Many insisted that what was needed was more effective economic aid, so that the Vietnamese could see that democracy brought greater prosperity than communism. The most popular exposition of this point of view was contained in *The Ugly American*.[15]

With John F. Kennedy's installation in the presidency in January 1961 the pace quickened. Kennedy enunciated the doctrine of the 'New Frontier' and announced that wherever freedom was threatened the United States would respond. His first unfortunate adventure was the attempted invasion of Cuba by C.I.A. hirelings, quickly overwhelmed by Castro's troops in the Bay of Pigs fiasco. Of more long-lasting consequence was his decision to send the American marines to Thailand in response to violations of the ceasefire in Laos which had followed the Geneva agreement. For the first time, the United States was totally committed; not just by providing advisers or cloak-and-dagger C.I.A. operators but by actually mustering ground combat troops in the Indo-China theatre.

American dissatisfaction with President Diem intensified, and in 1963 Diem was murdered in a military coup allegedly promoted by the C.I.A. with Kennedy's direct approval at a cost of $U.S. 20 million.[16] Kennedy was assassinated a few days after Diem, and the new President, Lyndon Johnson, found the administration committed to Americanising the war. He obtained a blank cheque from Congress through the Gulf of Tonkin resolution (1964) and thereafter the numbers of American troops in South Vietnam rose steadily until they stood at 520,000 in 1968. These were additional to the army of South Vietnam (600,000 men), and foreign troops brought in to fight (50,000 from South Korea, and smaller numbers from Thailand, the Philippines, Australia and New Zealand) like the Hessians hired by George III to fight against Washington's army.

The lesson which Vietnam had for Asia and Africa was that the American people – those who had 'fired the shot heard round the world' which began the process of revolution – were now the arch-imperialists, the suppressors of revolution. The Americans, who continued to preach their message of democracy, never understood that to the black and brown nations they were now the symbol of white oppression.

As the countryside became increasingly devastated by American bombing and raiding, more and more Vietnamese moved into Saigon which became a gigantic tourist centre catering for the American troops. Hundreds of American deserters settled in the city, opening bars and gambling-joints and taking Vietnamese wives. A great many American soldiers also acquired temporary Vietnamese mistresses. The orphanages were filled with children whose unknown fathers were Americans – white or black. A feverish atmosphere enveloped the city which had become a vicious parody of the American way of life. To a lesser extent, Bangkok, Singapore and Hong Kong were also corrupted by the frenzied search of the young American servicemen for an escape from the war. A great tide of resentment and hatred welled up against this crude American exploitation of South-east Asian cities and peoples. The Americans did not seem to care.

What Americans did understand was that the massive call-up of conscripts was causing an internal crisis in their country. At first, middle-class youths avoided the draft by going to college, or by getting married. As the regulations were tightened, they endeavoured to get away to universities abroad or to obtain exemption by declaring their opposition to the war. Working-class whites, and almost all blacks, were unable to opt out in these ways, so that a high proportion of the Americans in Vietnam – especially in the fighting units – were blacks, along with poor southern whites. Gradually, the draft began to affect suburban, middle-class, White America. Now came the era of campus protest; sincere, without doubt, but only aroused after the college students became personally exposed to the octopus of conscription. While unprecedented numbers of Americans were getting involved in Vietnam, something like an emotional civil war was tearing America itself apart. When in April 1970 President Nixon sent American forces into Cambodia there was a nationwide student protest of violent dimensions. At Kent State University the National Guard fired upon the students, killing four. By now, it was clear that if the United States was destroying Vietnam by air bombing heavier than throughout the whole of the Second World War, by the defoliation of its forests and the massacre of its people (as at My Lai), then also Vietnam was destroying the United States.

Gradually, the American army in Vietnam began to fall apart. The incidence of drug-taking was higher than among equivalent age groups in the United States, and indeed drugs were treated as a normal part of the combatant soldier's life, in order to counteract tension and fear. The black soldiers separated themselves from their white counterparts, wearing Black Power insignia and giving Black Power salutes instead of the normal salute (though they rarely saluted their white officers). The American army had become 'integrated' at the time of the Korean War, abandoning the old segregated units, but once again the army was dividing into black and white; with a new sense that they were on opposing sides, for increasingly black leaders declared that they would not fight a war for the white men against the Vietnamese people.

President Nixon had promised the American voters he would end the war with a victory over communism; instead it was obvious that the war must be ended on any terms possible. Negotiations with the Viet Cong and with North Vietnam opened in Paris in May 1968, but a ceasefire agreement was not concluded until January 1973. By then, many American soldiers had been withdrawn, and after the agreement they all departed. From the American standpoint, the last remaining objective was to secure the release of American prisoners of war. When they were returned in February, Vietnam ceased to dominate the television screens of America.

A high price had been paid. The Communist forces were holding their own recognised zones in South Vietnam, and within two years the military regime, propped up for so long by mountainous American military aid, abruptly collapsed. The Communists took over, renaming Saigon as Ho Chi Minh city.

At the last moment there was a scramble to get out by those Vietnamese identified as American collaborators: and also by hundreds of others caught up in the mood of panic. About 12,000 were admitted into the United States and a few (mainly orphans) came to Britain and other countries. Then America turned its back upon Vietnam. Unlike the 'loss' of China, this much more real loss, costing so much in American lives and American public money and American prestige, brought no witch-hunt in the United States. Too many leading Americans had been involved in the tragic misadventure. And the lesson was too painful: brown men could defeat white men, even when the whites had all the big guns and the big bombs.

Beside the American defeat in Vietnam the French withdrawal from Algeria was less obviously a world disaster, and yet for a time it appeared as though it might destroy both Algeria and France. The crisis came in 1958 when French military leaders, in conjunction with the European population of Algiers and Oran, rebelled endeavouring to overthrow the French government (see Map 1). The crisis was resolved by the return of de Gaulle as President, putting all his immense prestige behind finding a solution. The war in Algeria dragged on, with the same brutality as in Vietnam, and the same mobilisation of brown men to fight other brown men at the orders of white officers. Finally, in 1962 the Algerian nationalists won: at a cost of 1½ million dead in a nation of 11 million. Agreement was reached upon a procedure whereby France withdrew and recognised the F.L.N. (*Front de Libération Nationale*) as the government. The new situation involved the departure of most of the white colonists who had lived in Algeria for generations and were known to the metropolitan French as *pieds noirs*. Uneasily, they tried to make a new life; many settling in Corsica. The thousands of Algerians who had fought in the French army against the F.L.N. could not be abandoned, and like the Ambonese they went into exile into the homeland of their European masters. Algerians had long gone to France as temporary workers, filling an essential role in the construction industry and other sectors demanding cheap manpower. After Algeria became independent, French sentiment turned against the Algerians and they paid for their country's independence by becoming outcasts in France, liable to be set upon at any time, or even murdered, without the French police feeling any kind of responsibility.

Vietnam and Algeria were the only countries which overthrew Western colonialism by a prolonged armed struggle, but in important ways their struggle was reflected in the attitude of other Third World countries to the West. Algeria and Vietnam demonstrated that the façade of Western imperialism was vulnerable. Between 1945 and 1970, Western imperialism – white dominance – came to an end everywhere, except in the southern extremity of Africa. Brown men absorbed the lesson that the white metropolitan strongholds were vulnerable too, and after the jungle fighter was to come the urban guerrilla.

4 The End of Empire

WHEN the United Nations emerged as an international association for peace in October 1945, 51 states were admitted to membership. Of these member-states, 3 were Asian (India, China, the Philippines), 2 were African (Ethiopia and Liberia) and 7 belonged to the Middle East. The great majority were the countries of Europe (including the U.S.S.R.), the Americas, and the White Commonwealth countries.* By December 1971, after the People's Republic of China was at last admitted to membership of the U.N., there were 132 member-states, of whom 70 per cent belonged to the Third World. The entire atmosphere of the U.N. and of international politics had changed: and this change had come about as the result of the dissolution of all the Western empires.

The principal act of decolonisation was the phasing out of the British Empire. In 1947–8, Britain relinquished control over five important imperial possessions. Then came a pause, and in 1956–7 three more colonial possessions became independent. There was another short pause, and in 1960, with independence for Nigeria and Cyprus, the main decolonisation process got under way. Within another ten years every colony within the British Empire which demanded its freedom was allowed to go (see Table: 'New Nations').

The only important territory to remain under British control was Hong Kong, together with a number of small Caribbean islands which opted for 'associated status', and a few remaining strategic outposts such as Gibraltar, St Helena, the Falkland Islands and Diego Garcia.

Thus, the British Empire – which had been over three hundred years in growing (from the founding of Virginia in 1607 to the assumption of

* India's membership stemmed from previous membership of the League of Nations: India was under British rule until 1947, though at the second meeting of the General Assembly, 1946, Nehru's sister, Mrs Pandit, was the principal Indian delegate and a nationalist voice was heard. The Philippines was a U.S. colony in 1945 also. Although the big powers dominated the early U.N., the Latin Americans formed the largest single group – 17 – and small states like Dominica, Guatemala, Nicaragua, Honduras (all then under strong American influence) assumed an artificial importance.

New Nations
(formerly portions of the British Empire)

Date of Independence

1947	India, Pakistan
1948	Burma, Ceylon, Israel
1956	Sudan
1957	Gold Coast (Ghana), Malaya (1963 Malaysia)*
1960	Nigeria, Cyprus
1961	Tanganyika, Sierra Leone
1962	Uganda, Jamaica, Trinidad
1963	Kenya, Zanzibar (incorporated in Tanzania 1964)
1964	Malta, Malawi, Zambia
1965	Singapore (ex Malaysia), the Gambia
1966	Botswana, Lesotho, Barbados, Guyana
1967	Aden (Yemen)
1968	Mauritius, Swaziland, Nauru
1970	Fiji, Tonga
1975	Papua–New Guinea†

* In 1963, Sarawak and British North Borneo were also joined to Malaya to form Malaysia, which included Singapore for two years, 1963–5.

† Previously owned by Australia.

Mandates under the League of Nations in 1919) took about twenty years to liquidate.[1] The first phase – from the transfer of power to India in 1947 to the handover in the Gold Coast (Ghana) in 1957 – can be called the period of planned decolonisation, when deliberate preparations were made for transferring power, by training a national élite (politicians, civil servants, military officers) who had some experience in the arts of government and administration. During this phase there was also some effort to make the new nations economically viable, by equipping them with central banks and ensuring they had overseas balances to finance future development. Then came the second phase, in which almost the sole precaution was to identify an accepted national leader to whom power could be transferred. In many ways this was the pattern as early as 1948 when Burma's bid for independence succeeded largely because Aung San, and later U Nu, stood out as undeniable leaders. The last, ignominious episode came in Aden, where British forces pulled out leaving whoever could lay claim to power to make his claim effective:

> The good old rule,
> Sufficeth them, the simple plan,

> That they should take, who have the power,
> And they should keep who can.

The acceleration to independence in the British Empire from 1960 onwards was partly the result of internal developments in British politics: the Conservatives, who governed Britain from 1951 to 1964, suddenly altered course after Harold Macmillan's celebrated 'Winds of Change' speech. But more important was the shift in the world view. Quite suddenly, from colonies having been symbols of power and prestige they became symbols of backwardness and reaction. The year 1960 was the *annus mirabilis* in which seventeen new states entered the United Nations; and all were new nations in Africa (including Madagascar). Britain's new colonial policy reflected this shift in the world balance.

Right from the start of the process, each move towards a transfer of power served to reinforce divisions between communities within the countries scheduled for nationhood. In India, the demand by Muslim leaders for a separate state for the Indian Muslims brought about the division of the sub-continent which, if not mutually acceptable, was at any rate accepted. In Palestine, the insoluble divisions between Arabs and Jews prevented any acceptable Palestinian agreement. The new U.N. proposed a plan for partition (endorsed both by the U.S.A. and by the U.S.S.R.) but the Arabs turned it down, and the British withdrew from a Palestine which was already being disputed between the Jews and their Muslim and Christian neighbours who were now enemies. And so began the conflict which almost thirty years later is no nearer to an acceptable solution. In Burma, the ethnic minorities – especially the Karens – demanded their own separate states and, despite attempts to pacify them by a quasi-federal constitution, the ethnic minorities one by one revolted against the central government. Even in peaceable Ceylon, the Sinhalese majority moved towards a confrontation with the Tamil minority communities.

In East and Central Africa the situation was complicated by the presence of white settler communities – not numerous enough to compose a dominant minority (as in South Africa, where the whites are approximately one-quarter of the total population), but strong enough, as a result of the position established under British colonial rule, to impress Whitehall that they must be appeased (see Map 1). The formula put together was that of 'multi-racialism' or partnership between black and white. Unfortunately, the Prime Minister of

Southern Rhodesia, Sir Godfrey Huggins, chose to illustrate the nature of this partnership by likening it to that of a rider and his horse. The plan gradually emerged for a federation in Central Africa among self-governing Southern Rhodesia and the two colonial territories of Northern Rhodesia and Nyasaland.

From the beginning, articulate African opinion was flatly opposed to the plan, but the British government set up the Central African Federation in 1953 after a vote in favour by a referendum, mainly of white voters. The new federal legislature was composed of twenty-nine Europeans and six Africans, and all effective power was in European hands. The Federation lasted for ten years. During this period, there was no further advancement by Africans towards a fuller share in the government of this land in which the whites numbered only one in every twenty-five of the population.

Population Distribution of the Central African Federation 1960 (estimated)

	White	Black	Coloured
Southern Rhodesia	223,000	2,830,000	16,300
Northern Rhodesia (Zambia)	76,000	2,340,000	10,300
Nyasaland (Malawi)	9,300	2,810,000	12,800

After growing African agitation, the Federation was dissolved in 1963, and the following year Zambia and Malawi attained independence with black majority rule (see Map 2). White Rhodesians claimed the same status, but London refused; independence for Southern Rhodesia was made conditional on Africans receiving a larger share in the government. Frustrated, the white Rhodesians (who had inherited most of the Federation's defence forces and equipment) declared their own independence: U.D.I. (Unilateral Declaration of Independence). To their chagrin, no other country – not even South Africa – recognised their regime. The United Nations condemned U.D.I. and an economic blockade was imposed, which all member-nations were supposed to uphold. Economic advantage proved stronger than political principle. The list of sanction-breakers included nearly all the main trading nations: France, Germany, U.S.A., U.S.S.R., Japan, as well as several African states.

Elsewhere, in British East Africa, the multi-racial formula was invoked by white settlers to preserve some of their power and influence.

It made no appeal to Africans. The first outburst of militant African nationalism came with the Mau Mau rebellion – at its height from 1952 to 1956. Mau Mau was stigmatised as a tribal aberration, and Kenyatta was interned as one implicated in murderous and beastly practices; though afterwards it was all interpreted as a struggle by the Kikuyu to recover their lands. The whites and the Africans seemed even further apart. Within five years they had agreed to co-operate. The Kenya white settlers (55,759 compared to 8,365,942 Africans) acquiesced in their own political extinction after the British government set up a fund to guarantee the purchase of their farms at commercial prices. Taking away their ample compensation, most of the white Kenyans headed for South Africa. The British government offered no compensation to the Kenya Asians (176,613), but they were assured that all who held British passports would be freely admitted into the United Kingdom.

Elsewhere, the independence march was interrupted or halted by ethnic divisions which appeared stronger than any sense of shared nationhood. When the British decided to speed up the transfer of power in Malaya, to provide evidence that those opposing communism could 'deliver the goods' of independence just as well as the Communist guerrillas, they handed over to a government mainly composed of Malay aristocrats, supported by some Chinese business leaders. Then arose the question of the future of Singapore, and of the British territories in Borneo. The logical solution appeared to be to join these territories with Malaya in an enlarged Malaysia. However, Singapore is essentially a Chinese city, and Singapore politics is led by a group of dynamic, modern politicians who are Chinese though they plan to develop a new, urban style of politics based upon a greater share-out for all. Their leader, Lee Kuan Yew, coined the slogan 'For a Malaysian Malaysia', by which he meant the liquidation of the old-style alliance between Malay and Chinese vested interests. The Prime Minister of Malaysia, Tungku Abdul Rahman, observed this development with alarm. Very soon, he decided that Lee posed a threat to Alliance politics (which he conceived as letting in communism) and so Lee Kuan Yew's Singapore was required to leave Malaysia. The ethnic proportions of these different combinations are significant (see Table overleaf).

It is evident that the agreement to include Singapore in Malaysia had the effect of transforming the Malays into a minority, while the decision to exclude the island made the Malays the largest community once again. Unhappily, the minority complex which pervaded all the communities still persisted; and when the general election of 1969

Population Distribution: Malaya, Singapore, Malaysia
(Percentages)

	Malays	Chinese	Indians	Others
Malaya				
(without Singapore)	50·1	36·8	11·1	2·0
Singapore	15·0	76·2	7·0	1·8
Malaysia 1				
(with Singapore)	40·6	42·2	9·4	7·8
Malaysia 2				
(without Singapore)	45·9	35·7	9·6	8·8

proved a setback to the Malay-dominated Alliance government and a gain to the mainly Chinese Leftist parties there was a communal explosion. The country was again put under the 'Emergency' type of rule, and democratic politics languished while the remnants of the Communist guerrillas on the Thai – Malaysian border received a new lease of popular support.

The uneasy rivalry between communities perceiving themselves as separate and different has affected the pace of political development in a number of smaller states. In Guyana and Mauritius there are majority communities of Indian origin, and minorities – the Creoles – who are mainly of African origin with a European admixture. In Guyana, independence was delayed because the Indian leader Cheddi Jagan – whose People's Progressive Party scored three election victories within eight years – was labelled as a Communist. Thanks largely to American objections, Jagan was denied all his demands and a system of proportional representation was devised in Whitehall which gave a tenuous majority to an anti-Jagan coalition led by the Negro, Forbes Burnham. Burnham was awarded the independence refused to Jagan, and after independence by manipulating the electoral machinery he assured himself of permanent power. Thus, in Guyana the regime is supported by the black minority who provide the bulk of Burnham's security forces. Much the same tactics were tried by Creole politicians in Mauritius, encouraged by the sugar interests, but the shrewd old Indian leader of the island's Labour Party, Ramgoolam, was not to be toppled over. By cautious tactics he preserved the Labour Party in power, and took Mauritius into independence. By introducing Indians into the administration and into the security forces he gave his authority a firm foundation.

Fiji, one of the last British colonies to move into independence, also has a mixed population with Indians outnumbering the Melanesian Fijians. As in Malaya, the aristocrats of Fijian race are wise in the arts of government, and under Sir Kamisese Mara they achieved a smooth transition from an autocratic to a democratic style of government without relaxing their hold over affairs. However, Mara has governed in a more relaxed fashion than the Malay premiers, and by extolling 'the Pacific way' as one of goodwill he has given credence to the image of multi-racialism, both politically and socially in Fiji. Confrontation has been avoided by co-operation.

Multi-racialism was the keynote of Commonwealth politics during the 1950s and 1960s when the successful adaptation from Empire to Commonwealth was made. Initially, there was the existing reality of the small 'White Commonwealth' of those Dominions where emigrants from Britain and Europe had settled. As we have seen, their tradition was one very firmly exemplified by a White Australia. Also, they continued to nurture close ties with Britain; they firmly supported the British monarchy, and they had hastened to stand beside Britain in fighting two world wars (New Zealand suffered heavier battle casualties, per head of male population, than any other nation in the Second World War).

When the new states of South Asia became independent in 1947–8 this family atmosphere could not continue on the old basis. Nehru and the leaders of India believed that they had wrested independence out of a 'freedom struggle' and this had to be completed by the new India renouncing the allegiance of the British crown and becoming a republic. The old Dominions managed to swallow this innovation and a formula was devised whereby King George VI still remained Head of the Commonwealth. Also, on the initiative of India the old link between the peoples of the different portions of the Empire – Commonwealth, which had been provided by all being subjects of the British Crown – British subjects – was modified so that the term 'Commonwealth citizen' could be employed as an alternative. Britain, and also Canada and India, adopted the new practice; other White Dominions postponed any change. A further Indian proposal that the citizenships of all the independent Commonwealth members should be interchangeable on the basis of a mutual Commonwealth citizenship was summarily dismissed by Canada, Australia and South Africa which had no intention of altering their immigration and citizenship laws to meet a demand for theoretical equality.[2]

The accommodation of India as a republic inside the Com-

monwealth was the most important factor in giving the association a
new lease of life. India became a republic in 1950 and was followed by
Pakistan (1956) and Ghana (1960). No other Commonwealth state
sought early republican status (Ceylon obtained assent to the change in
1956 but did not become a republic until 1972). Although most of the
newly independent states were to adopt a republican constitution, the
fourth member to follow this course – South Africa – contrived thereby
to exclude itself from Commonwealth membership. Because of the
precedent set up by India, it was the convention that a state seeking
republican status must first consult with the other member-states. In
1961, a referendum of the South African electors (overwhelmingly
white) produced a narrow majority for a republic in South Africa.
When this was put to the other prime ministers there were some, led by
Nehru, who insisted that continuing membership must depend upon
the liberalisation of South Africa's race laws. Premier H. F. Verwoerd
replied that to accept an ultimatum from other states on internal
policies was inconsistent with independence: hence, his country would
withdraw from the Commonwealth. Nehru told the Indian Parliament:
'Thereby, the question of racial equality has been put to the highest
level in the world context', but he had to acknowledge that apartheid
was not thereby weakened: 'The evil continues, and will continue in an
aggravated form. . . . The policies under which vast numbers of
Africans, as well as people of Indian descent suffer in South Africa are
continuing.'[3]

Largely because of the almost accidental withdrawal of South Africa,
the rapidly expanding Commonwealth continued to enjoy popularity
and esteem amongst its members. The words 'multi-racial Commonwealth' were on all lips, as though this was a talisman, evoking a
brotherhood of equality. In reality, although there was a full recognition of equality of status between member-states, large and small,
affluent and poor, there was no move towards a recognition of the
equality of peoples. Indeed, by a painful paradox, within twelve
months of South Africa's departure, Britain introduced the first law
entailing the exclusion of Commonwealth citizens, aimed unequivocally at black and brown Commonwealth peoples from the Caribbean
and South Asia.

However, all appeared to go well until the Rhodesian U.D.I. in 1965.
The new African member-states regarded Rhodesia as an affront to the
whole multi-racial concept; an attempt to reassert a white dominance
which was everywhere else passing away. Paradoxically, they assumed

that Britain as the mother country had the capacity, as well as the responsibility, to intervene and overthrow the illegal regime. But Harold Wilson had just become Prime Minister and Britain was entering that last long phase in which the Land of Hope and Glory shrivelled into a Wasteland.

In 1962 Dean Acheson produced his famous aphorism – that 'Britain has lost an empire and has not yet found a role' – and was greeted with indignation by British listeners. Within a few short years it became obvious that Acheson was not giving an opinion – merely stating a fact. Yet, to many of the new states which had so very recently regarded the Union Jack and all it stood for with so much awe, the new reality was difficult to grasp. At successive conferences of Commonwealth prime ministers, the Africans arraigned Britain for failing to do its duty concerning Rhodesia. A marked division occurred between Britain (and to a lesser extent Australia and New Zealand) as against the countries of the 'New' Commonwealth. It was noticed that in the white countries the argument that the whites of Rhodesia were their 'kith and kin' was frequently employed by politicians and others on the Right. As in the 1920s and 1930s, the unposed question was again whether there was an inner circle, the white family (in which even the illegal rulers of Rhodesia might claim membership), whereas the black and brown member-states were still regarded as the lesser breeds. As time passed and nothing changed in the status of the illegal regime in Rhodesia some of the heat apparently disappeared from the debate. The decision to move the meeting-place of the prime ministers from London to other Commonwealth capitals – Ottawa, Singapore and Kingston, Jamaica – also helped to shift the emphasis away from direct confrontation between Britain and the New states into a wider concern for all the problems of the Third World. The Commonwealth survived; but as a soft-centre organisation.

After the disastrous French experience in Vietnam and Algeria de Gaulle reversed the former hard-line policy towards the colonies. In Africa, there was an attempt to bind the former empire to France by forming very small units – mini-states – as the successor regimes.* (see Map 2). In 1958, de Gaulle presented a plan for these states to become

---

* The population of some of the newly formed African states was as follows: Gabon, 421,000; Mauritania, 725,000; Congo (Brazzaville), 795,000; Central African Republic, 1,177,00; Senegal, 2,550,000; Chad, 2,600,000. The largest were Upper Volta, 4,000,000 and the Malagasy Republic (Madagascar), 5,184,000. Compare Nigeria, 39,000,000 and Ghana, 7,000,000.

members of a French Community of Nations, with an elaborate organisational structure. Most of them agreed; but Guinea, led by a radical President, refused membership and chose independence. Two years later, all the other ex-colonies followed Guinea and the Community was dissolved. However, France was still able to bind them to her, by continuing to provide massive instalments of aid, as well as administrative and technical services. The E.E.C. was persuaded to provide an aid programme, and this was almost all channelled into the former French possessions. Moreover, France was successful in perpetuating the belief that culture meant only French culture. Universities and institutes in all the new states continued to be appendages of French higher education. The intellectual or inspirational concept of *Francophonie* was a good deal more successful than the political experiment of the Community. By concentrating flattering attentions upon the governing élites of the new states, France appeared to retain their devotion to French ideals.

France also preserved vestiges of the old empire intact. The sugar colonies – Martinique, Guadeloupe, French Guiana and Réunion acquired the status of *départements* of the *métropole*, electing deputies to serve in Paris. Their economies – dependent wholly upon the production of sugar – were totally subordinate to France. Réunion, far away in the Indian Ocean, even imports flowers and shellfish from France (along with everything else). *La Patrie* is still supposed to be France to the descendants of the African slaves and of indentured Indian labourers who form the mass of the population. There were also a few remaining colonies, like Jibuti on the Red Sea, preserved like fossil relics of a bygone age.

The United States was even more successful in binding its territorial possessions closely to the *métropole*. Because, according to the American legend, there had never been any colonies there could be no decolonisation. The Philippines had been under American 'tutelage' (which was somehow different) and independence was restored on 4 July 1946. Besides being presented with the American Independence Day, the Filipinos were also presented with a constitution and government which was a detailed duplicate of the American model. As a condition of formal independence, the Philippines was required to permit the United States to retain its own bases – naval dockyards, airfields, cantonments for troops – in different parts of the islands. These bases were to be held by the United States for one hundred years – until 2046. In addition, the Philippines were firmly tied to the American fiscal and tariff structure and its economy was that of an American satellite.

Not until President Marcos abrogated the constitution in 1970 did things begin to change. There were symbolic changes: thus, Independence Day was altered to 12 June, when the patriot Aguinaldo had proclaimed a Filipino republic in 1898. Marcos spoke also of changing the institutions of government, but this was a slower process. Meanwhile the Americans held on firmly to all their bases.

The other colonial territories did not acquire even this degree of freedom (except for Okinawa, taken from Japan in 1945[4]). Alaska and Hawaii were incorporated into the Union as the forty-ninth and fiftieth states. Alaska has an indigenous population of Eskimos, Aleuts and Amerindians, who form about 15 per cent of the total population; the remainder being almost all white immigrants (from the U.S.A., Canada, etc.). The indigenous population of Hawaii, the Hawaiians, are almost extinct, forming only 1·7 per cent of the present population. About 14·5 per cent are part-Hawaiian (in an earlier age they were labelled half-castes) and 32 per cent are white immigrants from North America. The remainder are Asian immigrants – the Japanese being the largest group (32·2 per cent), followed by the Filipinos (10·8 per cent) and Chinese (6 per cent). Hawaii remains part of the Pacific, not part of the United States – whatever the formal, constitutional set-up. Hawaii, like Fiji, has managed to follow the friendly 'Pacific way', though the more abrasive style of race relations prevalent in the *métropole* is filtering into the islands: even though the repressed Negroes form only 0·8 per cent of the population (and these are mainly temporary residents, members of the armed services).

There still remains a large number of territories which are colonies in any sense of that term, yet in American eyes are seen as 'Outlying Areas' (which is their official designation). They are administered by the Department of the Interior. Nevertheless, these unacknowledged colonies contain a population of 3 million and cover an area of 5000 square miles. The largest is Puerto Rico, a Spanish-speaking island in the Caribbean, which is designated a 'Commonwealth' – meaning that it has internal self-government – but is subordinate to Washington (Puerto Ricans have no share in electing the American President, neither do they have representatives in Congress). The strangest colony is the Canal Zone in Panama. Twenty years after the British pulled out of their Suez Canal base, the Americans are still firmly installed in Panama – their link between the Atlantic and the Pacific. However, the paramount need to present a 'good neighbour' image to Latin

America may bring to an end this imperial anomaly. The rest of America's colonies – the Virgin Islands, Samoa, Guam, Wake, etc. – are likely to be kept quiet by handouts until such time as their continuing retention becomes politically embarrassing to the United States.

Then what of America's 'invisible empire', those seemingly sovereign states which are really fiefs of the C.I.A. and the State Department? We just do not know how far Chile, Brazil and other Latin-American countries are in the grip of the United States. 'Project Camelot' was really only a minor instance of how the United States hires and trains those who can be helpful to the U.S.A. in Latin America. The project (supposedly research) was funded by the American army to the extent of $U.S. 6 million before its ramifications were exposed.[5] And yet, as the C.I.A. and other American agencies reinforce the control of the United States over Latin America, these activities stimulate a further escalation of resistance. A noticeable feature of the late 1960s and 1970s is the growing consciousness of the young and the radical-minded that their continent is part of the Third World. Only Cuba has emerged as a country fully identified with Africa and the Arabs; yet in almost every other country there are left-wing resistance movements – the urban guerrillas – whose first target is American imperialism. There is a savage polarisation of forces, and the right-wing regimes supported by the United States have strongly counter-attacked. The struggle will be very long.

To an even greater extent than America, the Soviet Union has been successful in removing its vast internal empire from the controversies surrounding decolonisation. The U.S.S.R. has its satellites in Eastern Europe and in Central Asia (Outer Mongolia), as well as its own non-Russian territories – Siberia and the Central Asian republics and the Far-Eastern seaboard, extending to the island of Sakhalin. All these areas were in former times portions of other empires (the Chinese and Japanese empires) or were independent states, such as Christian Armenia or the Islamic khanates. Even Siberia – which was so similar to the American West – was inhabited by semi-nomadic, indigenous peoples. The cry for independence, so loudly heard everywhere else, is muffled throughout these lands.* Their political future is settled forever: as constituent parts of the Soviet Union. Even better: the

---

* Georgia appears to exhibit more signs of national resentment than other republics. There have been isolated bombings, while on another plane the national claims of Georgian historians have been officially condemned.

U.S.S.R. has frequently succeeded in convincing the Third World that it is in some sense a part of Asia and has been admitted to membership of Third World organisations. There have been Soviet representatives at the meetings of the Afro-Asian Peoples' Solidarity Organisation (A.A.P.S.O.) and some Asian states have pressed for their attendance at other conferences of the non-aligned nations.

And so the Soviet Union marches on; the great exception to the disappearing Western empires. Two other small European colonial powers looked as though they, too, would hold out against the prevailing tide: Belgium and Portugal. Both suddenly moved from a position of 'no surrender' to 'instant surrender'.

It appeared as though Belgium would continue to administer the vast basin of the Congo, with its wealth of natural products, without reference to the age of decolonisation. Belgian policy had carefully refrained from creating a colonial élite through higher education and participation in the administration (as occurred in other colonies) and the Belgians calculated that they could somehow insulate their rich possession from the pressures of the outside world. Quite suddenly, they reversed this policy and decided on independence for the Congo overnight (see Map 2). Perhaps the calculation was that the Africans would be helpless, and would turn to Belgium for continuing support. The tragic leader Patrice Lumumba emerged to power. He was not permitted to govern for long. The Congo became a cockpit of intrigue in which the great powers – the U.S.S.R., the U.S.A. and others – manoeuvred and promoted their protégés.

The United Nations was invoked, and military forces from non-aligned states such as Tunis, India, Ireland and the new African states came in to preserve order.[6] Large areas were reduced to chaos and black zealots often fought it out with white mercenaries. Many Europeans remained in remote settlements when Belgium withdrew its control; some were Christian missionaries, others were planters and mining executives. There were much-publicised killings of these isolated whites by black commando forces. Hastily, the U.N. organised rescue operations. Belgium sent in its paratroopers. Nobody proclaimed that it was strange that the outside world should react so strongly to the death of a handful of whites while accepting the deaths of hundreds or thousands of Africans in the same conflict with apparent apathy. For outside of places such as South Africa, racism is not an officially proclaimed ideology; it is almost unconscious. Nevertheless, events in the Congo in 1960–1 demonstrated again that concern about a white life has much more impact than any vague awareness that blacks also are human and mortal.

The Portuguese rearguard action was stubbornly prolonged. So long as the dictatorship of Salazar, and his successor, Caetano, could retain power there was no move towards concessions. Resistance to Portuguese rule was most powerful in Angola and Mozambique, where mass movements developed, fostered by support from the neighbouring African states and from China and the U.S.S.R. The first to emerge was the *Movimento Popular de Libertação de Angola* (M.P.L.A.), founded in 1956; the *Frente de Libertação de Moçambique* (FRELIMO) followed in 1962.[7] A large proportion of the Portuguese army and a substantial part of the national budget was committed to suppressing these revolts which soon attained the level of a guerrilla war. Among the most dynamic of the Portuguese commanders was General Spinola, yet it was he who returned home and aroused the nation to the need to come to terms with the resistance movements. In a double revolution, Portugal moved from fascist dictatorship towards a Leftist mobocracy. Independence was conceded to all Portugal's African possessions, and in Mozambique the FRELIMO leaders took over without opposition.

Angola's future was disputed by three main parties, supported variously by Zaire, Zambia, South Africa, China and the Soviet Union. It was Soviet support for the M.P.L.A., combined with their initially tenuous control over the capital and its surroundings, which enabled this group to gain the ascendancy. The opposing movements were able to depend upon military intervention by the South African army and by a motley band of white (mainly British) mercenary soldiers. These forces were pushed back by the intervention of Cuban troops, operating Soviet tanks and Soviet military aircraft. Within a short while, in the opening months of 1976, the Cuban allies of the M.P.L.A. had secured the whole of Angola. South Africa hastily withdrew its army, even from the frontier with South West Africa (Namibia) where a massive South-African-promoted dam and hydro-electric complex was surrendered to the M.P.L.A.

A *frisson* of fear swept across Southern Africa: if the Cuban soldiers could so swiftly transform the relative strength of forces in Angola, might they not threaten Rhodesia, and even South Africa itself?[8] The isolation of Rhodesia in 1976 was almost complete. With financial aid from Britain and the United States, Mozambique shut down the railway line over which Rhodesian exports had reached the outside world; thereafter, all depended on a single track taking the long haul down to Cape Town. Still, Prime Minister Ian Smith tried to keep the clock back to the time of empire. His decision to bring African chiefs into his government had all the ring of Cecil Rhodes. Henry Kissinger, and other white spokesmen warned that time had run out, and that white military aid would not be forthcoming if a race war developed in Rhodesia. Still Smith prevaricated, hoping that the deluge would not descend in his time.

Prime Minister Vorster of South Africa observed these events with apprehension. It was impossible for the white Rhodesians to avoid being labelled as colonial intruders; he still hoped that white South Africans would be accepted by black Africans as indigenous people in Africa (see Map 2). His recognition of the neighbouring African regimes of Botswana, Lesotho and Malawi, the granting of a form of independence to the Zulus and other African tribes in their 'Bantustans' – surely these would pay dividends? Vorster even began to hint that a form of independence might be accorded to Namibia (where the white population is only 12 per cent of the total). For here South Africa was on its weakest ground. The U.N. ruled that South Africa must terminate its mandate over South West Africa, and an appeal was lodged with the International Court at The Hague. The International Court first ruled that South Africa must accept its jurisdiction, but then reversed its own verdict (1965) when the Australian President by his casting vote declined to consider the case: to non-whites this was a racial decision. However, there was little support for continuing occupation, except among a dwindling number of sympathisers in West Germany and the Netherlands. Vorster was reluctantly prepared to pull back from his outer defences – Rhodesia and Namibia – if only Black Africa would recognise white rule in South Africa itself. The slogans of multi-racialism heard twenty years earlier in East and Central Africa now had a certain tinsel attraction. Ian Smith's Rhodesia looked less than impregnable by the summer of 1976, but it was clear that Vorster's South Africa would withstand all but the most determined assault. In the late 1970s, the long siege of South Africa had only just begun.

For the ninety states which have achieved independence since the Second World War – ranging from India, with a population representing about one-sixth of the world's people, down to the mini-states and the micro-states (such as the Maldive Islands or Bhutan) – the end of colonialism has involved the continuation of neo-colonialism. This term is most often used for the economic dependence which still prevails in all the new states (other than the oil producers). Yet the term also describes the political situation; for new states were created before new nations could emerge. Not all the new states inherited political structures so utterly imposed by an imperial donor as did the Philippines: but even when new constitutions were hammered out by constituent assemblies, the resulting apparatus always bore a strong resemblance to the institutions of the departed imperial power.

Gradually, this situation was challenged. Parliamentary democracy began to be labelled 'fifty-one per cent democracy' in countries frustrated by the manoeuvres of party politicians. Several states tried to break away from Western patterns, and in order to give more meaning to the electoral process introduced systems in which local people voted for local councillors – who in turn voted for a regional assembly which in turn elected the national assembly. This pyramid structure was an attempt to create political institutions in tune with Afro-Asian attitudes, instead of simply borrowing from the West.[9] Most of the new states struggled on with their inherited political institutions, which they applied to problems also inherited from the colonial period. The most insoluble problem was that of the 'plural society', defined by J. S. Furnivall in the context of Burma as forming 'A medley, for they mix but do not combine. Each group holds by its own religion, its own culture and language, its own ideas and ways. . . . There is a plural society with different sections of the community living side by side, but separately, within the same political unit.'[10] Writing in the twilight before decolonisation Furnivall hoped that the plural society might be knit together within a new national consciousness. The problem was to prove much more intractable.

In many situations from Burma to Biafra, the new states struggled against divisions within society, and fought against secession and disintegration. They continued to be the clients, the outsiders, in a world where the West (coinciding with the white 'over-developed' nations, plus Japan) seemed to hold all the important cards in the pack. However, the Afro-Asian world had one asset – even if an asset of dubious value – it had superiority in numbers. If the West could adopt a strategy of 'Betting on the Strong', the Third World could reply with the counter-strategy of 'Betting on the Many'.

The population explosion, of which so much is written, is actually the rapid expansion of the Third World while the West and the U.S.S.R. grow slowly or, like Britain, remain static in terms of population. It has been calculated that whereas in 1900 there was one European for every two Asians, by the year 2000 there will be only one European for every four Asians.[11] It is difficult not to see this change as pointing to the eventual decline of Europe.

It is in Asia that the spectacular change is happening. In 1950, the world population was 2509 million, and over half lived in Asia: 1380 million (excluding the Asian population of the U.S.S.R.). By comparison, the population of Africa was 199 million and of Latin America, 163 million: altogether their numbers were only one-quarter of the Asian total. By A.D. 2000 the world population on a 'medium' projection of growth will reach 6100 million. The population of Asia is expected to reach 3870 million while Latin America will attain 592 million and Africa 517 million.

It was apprehension of a dramatic shift in the balance of the world's peoples that led an earlier generation of white publicists to issue warnings of doom: such as T. L. Stoddard's *The Rising Tide of Colour Against White World Supremacy* (1920). Concern about the population explosion was first expressed in the United States, Sweden and other affluent countries. Would Asia and Africa 'invade' the West in a new, unimaginable mass migration? This subconscious fear contributed to putting the West on the defensive in the second half of the twentieth century.

5 A Defensive West

THE effect of surrendering their empires varied among the different European ex-colonial overlords. During the 1950s and early 1960s it appeared as though the most traumatic effect would be experienced by France. The loss of Vietnam and then Algeria led to a strong right-wing reaction. A phantom army was formed, the O.A.S. (*Organisation Armée Secrète*) which launched assassination attacks upon politicians denounced as traitors, and which terrorised Algerian and other immigrants. However, de Gaulle succeeded in demonstrating that France could still generate a special kind of world-prestige which appealed to Africans and Asians – and he even stirred the 'colonised' people of Quebec by the cry *Vive le Québec libre, vive le Québec Français*. France ceased to be neurotic about past imperial glories and established a new kind of hegemony within the European Community.

When the British left India they departed almost in a glow of euphoria with bands of the Indian army lustily playing them out with 'Auld Lang Syne' (though omitting 'Will ye no come back again'). The end of empire was cushioned by the belief that the British Empire had been transmuted and transmogrified into the British Commonwealth, which would be essentially the same thing. Only gradually did the realisation dawn that Britain's role in the new Commonwealth was quite different. Instead of being the mentor and accepted leader, Britain was often treated as the repentant sinner; the imperialist who had (rather late, perhaps) realised the error of former ways.

In 1956, Britain attempted to resume the old imperial role in the abortive Suez invasion. There was a storm of protest, in which Canada's voice was heard equally with that of India and Pakistan. Only Australia and New Zealand remained stubbornly loyal to the mother country. Suez was an aberration from which, it appeared, Britain adjusted very rapidly. The canal zone was quickly evacuated and the 'Special Relationship' with the United States – frozen into an iceberg throughout the Suez operation – was resumed. Yet things were never quite the same again. As one small instance: in the years before Suez, all the

Commonwealth representatives at the U.N. met together before meetings of the Assembly or the Security Council and informed each other how they intended to speak and vote. After Suez they never met again.

British disgruntlement after Suez was especially focused upon Nehru, who condemned Britain's action, but who spoke in muffled tones about the simultaneous invasion of Hungary by the Soviet Union. The racial basis of the old empire began to re-emerge in the attitude of British people to black and brown Commonwealth citizens, especially as they entered Britain. The enforced withdrawal of South Africa, and the isolation of Rhodesia after U.D.I. emphasised that white men were being pushed around by black men. A new party emerged in England, the National Front, calling for a different Commonwealth – a return to the family of white nations. The National Front was looked down upon by superior people; the Front scored its best election successes in London's East End. However, a leading Conservative, Enoch Powell, began to direct his attention to the consequences of mass immigration into Britain from the 'New' Commonwealth and his message was received with approval by many of the middle and upper classes. Racist sentiments, which before the 1960s were shunned by respectable people, could now be uttered in almost any circle.

For Belgium and the Netherlands, the loss of the empires which had made these little countries important was accepted in a spirit of realism. The status of any country was no longer measured by its overseas possessions but by the strength of its currency on the international money market: and the Belgian franc, with the Dutch guilder, were among the strongest currencies in the world. Britain's decline was assessed much more often by the falling pound than by the disappearing Union Jack.

As a practitioner of the new realism, none surpassed Japan. After the collapse of the Greater East Asia Co-Prosperity Sphere, Japan maintained a very low profile in international affairs. Japan's economic expansion in South-east Asia progressed methodically and with ever-increasing momentum. First, Japan offered reparations to countries which had suffered war damage as a consequence of the Japanese occupation (though this damage had been mainly caused by Allied artillery and bombers). It was discovered that there was little resentment, and Japan's recovery from the ashes of defeat was respected and envied. Even in Singapore, where perhaps one out of ten in the Chinese population had been liquidated by the *Kempeitai* (secret police), the Japanese were accepted and became important pioneers in the growth of new industries.

At the height of the Vietnam war it seemed as though the American people would be torn apart in the controversy about whether the war was a crusade for democracy or an unparalleled act of aggression and destruction. The American military – industrial – political complex was identified by radicals – and by liberals – as a closed circle of power whose aim was domination of the globe. The image of élitism and imperialism seemed to acquire its ultimate form. One President was destroyed by Vietnam. Lyndon Johnson, appalled at the consequences of his own decisions, withdrew from the power game. Another President, Richard Nixon, elected on a promise to win the war, finally acknowledged that the war could not be won and commissioned his Secretary of State to create a credible alternative.

The Nixon regime was shaken by the revelations concerning Vietnam contained in the Pentagon Papers, and was discredited by its efforts to destroy the source of the revelation. However, the long-drawn-out Watergate investigation of the extent to which an interior imperialism had been employed to manipulate and pervert the domestic political process provided a kind of purgation. When the United States pulled out of Vietnam it seemed that it was turning its back upon Manifest Destiny, and all that, forever. Finally, as the regime of President Thieu in South Vietnam collapsed like a house of cards, the only response was the rather grudging admission of Vietnamese refugees into the United States. The establishment of camps for the Vietnamese exhibited the United States at its best and its worst. Hundreds of volunteers came forward to help the refugees to take the enormous leap needed from the vanished world of South-east Asia into mainline America. At the same time, politicians and local leaders cried out that they had enough problems already with unemployment and crime and could not absorb the Vietnamese in *their* town.

The Vietnamese influx of 1975 was only the most dramatic example of how the consequences of Western imperial expansion have, in the aftermath of imperialism, unexpectedly arrived on the doorstep of the West.

The nineteenth century saw mass emigration from Europe to the New World of North America and Australasia. The nineteenth century also saw the more or less involuntary emigration of Asians to semi-tropical territories where, before, the African slave had built up the plantation economy. The second half of the twentieth century sees the mass emigration of black and brown people to shake up the old age of Europe as well as to disturb the middle age of America.

The explanation is not very complicated. The Third World remains desperately poor; the 'take-off into sustained growth', prophesied by Western economists for the 'developing' countries during the last twenty years, just has not occurred. During the same period, the working class in the West – now termed the blue-collar workers – have moved out of the lower-paid, dirty sectors of industry, or those sectors where long hours at awkward times of day have to be endured. Those older sectors, often still using nineteenth-century industrial techniques and processes, have been compelled to search far and wide for recruits. The most enterprising of the people of Asia, Africa and the Caribbean have come forward to supply the demand.

Countries where the *per capita* annual income is less than $200 (or £100) include India, Bangladesh, Pakistan, Sri Lanka, Kenya, Mali, Tanzania, Uganda, Ethiopia and Sudan (see Map 2). In all these countries the growth rate has never risen above 3 per cent per annum – barely enough to absorb the rise in population – and in the quinquennium 1973–8 there is stagnation or actual reduction in incomes. The next 'layer' of countries includes Egypt, Greece, Syria, Tunisia, Turkey, Yugoslavia, most of former French Africa, Korea, the Philippines, Thailand, Mexico and most of Latin America. The only truly developing countries in the Third World are the oil producers of the Middle East, Iran, Nigeria and Venezuela: where, very often, gross social inequalities restrict the spread of wealth (in addition to the migration into Western Europe and the United States a strong, new migration is flowing into the oil countries of the Middle East).

By contrast to this global sea of poverty, between 1960 and 1970 the rich countries of the world added $700 billion to their annual income. The difference between *per capita* incomes in western Europe and in Asia is now about $2000 per wage-earner: on current trends it will widen to $7000 by the end of the twentieth century. It is inevitable that the poor will seek to penetrate the rich societies, whether lawfully or unlawfully. Because the would-be immigrant from Asia or Africa will be more familiar with the ways of the former colonial power – he is likely to know at least a smattering of the former overlord's language – he attempts to make his way to that country first.

Control over new arrivals may be by two main methods. One is by laying down the legal conditions of entry in terms of nationality and citizenship. The other is by regulating the newcomer when he actually arrives by means of job permits and other labour documents, and by relying upon the police to pick up and expel all those who are unwanted.

In practice, all the Western nations have tended to concentrate upon the method of admitting those acceptable as supplementary workers while excluding, as far as possible, those who will not provide needed services. In conformity with the old nineteenth century tradition of liberalism in opposition to totalitarianism, most Western governments have continued to allow entry to those who can claim to be political refugees. It was on that basis that the Vietnamese were admitted to the United States in 1975 and the British Asians arrived from Uganda in 1972. Refugees from Communist Hungary and from fascist Chile have received a warmer welcome in the West, however. They are white, and more or less invisible.

During the 1960s and 1970s, the United States and Britain have increasingly coalesced in their policies, having begun from entirely opposed positions. Traditionally, Britons believed that they lived in a colour-blind country in which all British subjects were equal before the law. In addition, entry into Britain was open to everyone from the Empire – Commonwealth. Thus, British policy towards immigrants, including those who were black and brown, could be described as non-restrictive or *laissez-faire*. The United States, despite its pioneer tradition as the Land of the Free, had acquired a whole range of legal and social restrictions based upon race and colour affecting entry into the country, as well as internal restrictions upon the political and civil rights of many who were American citizens.

Gradually, the United States revised its immigration policy towards a much less overtly racial basis, while moving towards the attainment of more equal civil and political rights through government action and legislation. Britain gradually imposed greater restrictions on admission while (even more gradually) it was acknowledged that *laissez-faire* within British society had permitted a range of racial discrimination. If today the United States has more liberal policies and Britain has more restrictive and protective policies, the effect is to leave both countries more or less on a parity in their treatment of the lesser breeds.

*

The United States has a much larger proportion of 'colonised' peoples among its native-born population than Britain. According to the 1970

Census, the total population was 203,212,000. The non-white minorities numbered about 32 million or about one-sixth of the total population.

Non-white Minorities in the United States

Negro	22,600,000	11·1% of total
Mexican (Chicano)	5,000,000	2·2%
Puerto Rican	1,500,000	0·7% (N.B. residents of mainland)
Amerindian	793,000	0·39%
Japanese	591,000	0·29%
Chinese	435,000	0·21%
Filipino	343,000	0·12%
Other Asians	720,000	0·36% (Koreans, Indians, etc.)

Other groups also considered they formed minorities in the United States. The 6 million American Jews were a relatively identifiable community, but the 40 million lumped together under the label of the 'ethnics' (40 per cent of the total) comprised all the immigrants from Eastern and Southern Europe who supposedly had gone into the American melting-pot and emerged as one hundred per cent American. Yet it transpired that these formed the last great minority, 'the unmeltable ethnics'.[1]

Some among the non-white minorities, especially the Amerindians and the Negroes, are the oldest communities in North America. Those listed as Mexican – or *Chicano* as they term themselves – also include many whose ancestors settled in the vast south-west of the United States (then part of the territory of Spanish Mexico) decades, even centuries, before the 'Anglo' (as they term mainline Americans) came in as invaders. However, some of these Spanish-speaking *Chicanos* are recent immigrants from Mexico. Similarly, the Puerto Ricans and most of the Asian groups are relatively recent arrivals. The growth rate of different groups shows striking variations. During the decade 1960–70, American blacks increased by 19·7 per cent. The Amerindians increased by 51·4 per cent (due to their recovery from the previous wastage caused by disease and poverty). The Filipinos increased by 94·9 per cent during the decade, and this was due in great part to the changes in the immigration laws in the mid-1960s.

The new laws became partly effective in 1965, then after a transition period fully effective in 1968. The old quota system, giving heavy emphasis to north-west Europe, was abandoned. The total numbers allowed to enter in any year were raised from 150,000 to 290,000, of whom 120,000 admissions were assigned to the Western Hemisphere and 170,000 to immigrants from the rest of the globe. A total of 20,000 admissions was the most that any one country would receive (though this was not enforced in practice). Priority was given to persons with relatives in the U.S.A. and to persons with special skills (doctors, engineers, etc.). The result was a dramatic change in the national origins of immigrants. In 1965, the five nations providing the most immigrants were, in order, Canada, Mexico, Great Britain, Germany and Cuba. By 1970 the top five were Mexico, the Philippines, Italy, Cuba and Greece (just ahead of China). British immigrants were reduced to eighth place and Canadians to tenth. This transformation of the immigration system became less dramatic in the mid-1970s, when America's economic recession led to a severe cut in immigrant numbers and a certain return to previous sources of immigration. Many Asians found evidence in this setback of renewed discrimination against non-whites.

It has often been argued that this change in the immigration laws was part of a conscious policy on the part of the Democratic administration – on the initiative, first, of President Kennedy – to improve America's image in the eyes of the Third World. As new nations emerged, especially in Africa, the United States discovered that its claim to be the champion of freedom was received with heavy scepticism. One story which went the rounds in Africa was that when Vice-President Nixon (as he then was) attended the independence celebrations in Ghana he turned to his black neighbour at the dinner table to ask 'How does it feel to be free?' The reply came: 'I wouldn't know. I'm from Alabama.'

When African diplomats went for excursions outside Washington they were liable to be turned away from southern restaurants and hotels. The racial bias of the immigration quota was the subject of resentful comment. Dean Rusk declared in 1961, when he was Secretary of State, 'The biggest single burden that we carry on our backs in our foreign relations in the 1960s is the problem of racial discrimination here at home.' And so the demands of foreign policy began to have repercussions upon race relations within the United States. But not fast enough for most non-white Americans: James Baldwin, the black writer, exclaimed about discrimination in restaurants in 1960: 'At the rate things are going, all Africa will be free before we can get a lousy cup of coffee.'[2]

The condition of the American Negro was greatly affected by the continuing massive movement of black people out of the rural South into the northern cities. During the decade 1960−70 one-third of all the new arrivals in the cities were Negroes. By 1970, just under one-half of the black population lived outside the South, whereas in 1950 two-thirds were still down in the South. In four major cities there was actually a black majority: in Washington, D.C.; in Newark, New Jersey; in Gary, Indiana; and in Atlanta, Georgia. Among the 8 million population of the city of New York (1970) there were about 1,300,000 blacks and over one million immigrants from Puerto Rico. During the decade 1960−70, New York's white population declined by 592,000, while blacks and browns increased by 705,000. In the old centres of the cities, the blacks and Puerto Ricans pressed hard against the ethnics − Italians, Poles, Hungarians, Czechs − whose low incomes prevented them from joining the white exodus to the suburbs. The ethnics pushed back and were loudly accused of racist behaviour. One writer commented: 'Liberals have empathized more with nearly every group in American society than with the lower-middle-class white ethnics whom they have tended to think of as racists, militarists, and crypto-fascists. Since their arrival in America, Slavs and Southern Europeans have been made to feel stupid, ignorant, immoral and backward.'[3] And so the ethnics have responded to George Wallace and other politicians who call upon them to defend *their* America.

This partly northern white backlash followed a decade of activity combating segregation and discrimination in the South. The civil rights movement only acquired momentum after Kennedy had secured his narrow presidential victory because of newly recruited black support. Negroes had traditionally voted Republican − for the party of Abraham Lincoln. (Martin Luther King, Sr had always voted Republican prior to the Kennedy−Nixon contest.) Thereafter, whenever southern blacks, supported by northern white liberals, challenged the racist regimes in the southern states they were assured of backing from Washington. Federal marshals supervised the marches and sit-ins; more important, federal legislation was introduced, and the Civil Rights Act of 1964 (enacted after Kennedy's assassination) struck at discrimination in restaurants, hotels, sports arenas, parks, hospitals and schools. The Voting Rights Act of 1965 followed; outlawing all the devices invented throughout the South for preventing the black man from casting a vote. The South resisted strenuously: only in 1970 was the Mississippi law against racial inter-marriage set aside. The Civil Rights Act of 1968 made an attempt to tackle a more intractable problem: discrimination in housing. It has not been a spectacular success, and in the American idiom an 'integrated' neighbourhood is actually one in which all the inhabitants are black!

The means by which Negro leaders have tried to struggle against discrimination and poverty have altered in response to the success – or lack of it – which they perceive to have followed their efforts.* During the first civil rights phase, the emphasis was upon an appeal to the conscience of White America. Martin Luther King, Jr emerged as an all-American and internationally recognised figure (he was awarded the Nobel Peace Prize). The culmination of his efforts was the March on Washington in August 1963 which led directly to the Civil Rights Act of 1964. Thereafter, his campaigns were less immediately successful and the attack upon social and economic discrimination seemed to languish. When King was shot in April 1968 his death was celebrated by the sacking and burning of downtown Washington: it was the antithesis of all his striving for non-violence.

The next phase saw the assertion of black liberation and black nationalism. The spotlight was taken by Malcolm X who repudiated all connection with White America, embracing a new religion, that of Islam (in the form preached by the Black Muslims), and calling for a separate black society in America, and even a separate territorial black state. It was the so-called Black Power movement which excited the white backlash among the ethnics. The polarisation of racial attitudes in the inner city was a two-way polarisation: James Baldwin observed: 'Hatred must have a symbol. Georgia has the Negro and Harlem has the Jew.' Race relations in the American inner city became a battlefield.

There were many grievances crying out for remedy. Unemployment among Negroes – especially among black teenagers – was well over double the national average (among the teenagers it reached 50 per cent). Consequently, the black crime rate was disturbingly high, especially in the growing figures for mugging. However, spokesmen for the Negro community insisted that crime was partly the result of

---

* During the 1970s it became the convention to speak of non-white people as blacks. This appellation is not wholly accepted, even by black people in the United States. A survey ascertained that for 38 per cent, the preferred term remained that of *Negro*, while to only 11 per cent was it the term they liked least. The alternative most/least preferences were *Coloured*, 20 per cent/31 per cent, *Black*, 19 per cent/25 per cent *Afro-American*, 10 per cent/11 per cent. Milton L. Barron, 'Recent Developments in Minority and Race Relations', *The Annals* (Philadelphia, July 1975) p. 143.

persecution by the police and the courts. One-third of the prisoners in jail in America are black, and the record shows that they are given heavier sentences than whites for the same crimes. Before the death penalty ceased to be imposed in America, from 1930—66, of the 3857 persons executed, 54 per cent were Negroes.[4]

In an effort to oppose the oppression of the police—or the 'pigs' as they were increasingly called—the Black Panthers were founded to provide the black community with its own defence force. The Panthers advocated black independence, based upon cultural nationalism. They were strong advocates of Pan-Africanism as a movement to bring together the new Africa and the Afro-Americans in a common stand against white imperialism. However, the Panthers were also re-volutionaries, drawing heavily upon Marxist—Leninist ideology. The question of how far they could combine with white revolutionaries led to a schism among them.[5] Their destruction came, however, from what seemed to be a definite policy on the part of the authorities to wipe them out. The Panthers held stocks of arms (for the American Constitution, by its Second Amendment, declares 'The right of the people to keep and bear arms shall not be infringed'). In several cities the police moved in, calling on the Panthers to surrender their weapons. They refused and were besieged, until in most cases they were all shot dead. The Panthers' leaders went underground or took refuge overseas (like Eldridge Cleaver in Algiers). A series of arrests and trials followed. At first the Panthers were severely punished, but by the time Angela Davis stood trial a combination of American weariness and soul-searching over Vietnam, and a blaze of adverse international publicity provided strong-enough pressures for her acquittal.

There followed a period in which White America seemed to go back on the defensive. The Negroes pressed successfully for much larger admissions to colleges and universities where they demanded re-cognition of their own separate culture by programmes of black studies, black English, etc. This black offensive in the world of education produced several counter-offensives.* Other minorities also demanded their own programmes of studies. Asian—American Studies was put in

---

* It might be argued that one consequence of black agitation was a revival of a neo-Darwinian controversy about how far intelligence and ability were related to racial characteristics. When Arthur Jensen asserted, 'The number of intelligence genes seems to be lower, overall, in the black population than in the white' he started a controversy of international proportions. His original theory was stated in 'How Much Can We Boost IQ and Scholastic Achievement?', *Harvard Education Review*, XXXIX (1969). It was restated in *Educability and Group Differences* (New York, 1973).

the curriculum at Berkeley, to be duplicated in almost all major universities, while southwest ethnic studies of the *Chicano* culture were introduced at 150 institutions in Texas, New Mexico, Nevada, etc. These minority studies led in turn to demands for Slavic and Latin studies concerned with the history of the white ethnics — and also stimulated the demand for women's studies. At the end of it all, Negroes were beginning to suspect that black studies was a blind alley: for they derived no benefit in their economic plight from these courses.[6] In the mid-1970s, many black leaders could see that separatism was generating a strong backlash whereby other groups were claiming minority privileges and syphoning resources away from the black ghetto into other areas.

In frustration, many returned to the more laborious strategy of capturing positions of political power to claim a fuller share of the bounty of America. Black politicians tried to imitate the strategy of Irish, Italian and Jewish politicians in employing the grass-roots organisation of the Democratic Party to boost their own communities. Black mayors were elected in important cities, and increased numbers of black representatives were elected, in the states and to serve at Washington. (Between 1971 and 1974, the number of blacks elected to public office rose from 1000 to 3000, including 108 mayors of cities.)[7] These black gains were offset by white resistance. The policy of busing (or bussing) black students to schools in white neighbourhoods in order to promote integration, caused protest and riot by white ethnics in cities such as Boston. Busing equally stirred up controversy among black leaders. Many insisted that black kids should not be removed from their own environment. After the 1960s and 1970s, the United States could never be the same again. The American dream of integration and equality of opportunity was shattered.

Somewhat apart from the main struggle between opposed races in the cities, the Amerindians girded themselves for renewed battle with their white oppressors. Their plight was worse than that of the blacks (apart from a small élite of Amerindians who, because they appear to have no fear of heights, are employed in the erection of the steel frames of high-rise buildings and, as 'spidermen', earn high wages). In 1970, the suicide rate among Amerindians (always an indicator of misery and frustration) was twice the all-American average; the unemployment rate at 45 per cent was over eight times the national average. Being scattered and isolated — half of them still lived on reservations, while the others lived on the fringes of towns — they had difficulty in attracting public notice. Moreover, being members of more than 250 tribes they spoke with many voices. When in 1966 the American Indian Movement (AIM) was founded in Minneapolis by some urban Indians the tribal leaders looked on suspiciously. However, AIM made a strong appeal to the younger generation who responded to its campaign of militancy with ardour. By the occupation of Alcatraz island in 1969, the sit-in at the Bureau of Indian Affairs (1972), and the battle of Wounded Knee, South Dakota, in 1973, the Indians have given evidence of what the media describe as 'Red Power'. They demanded restitution from the American government for the lands and rights taken away in the past and the opportunity to manage their own society free of the paternalistic control of the Bureau of Indian Affairs. In certain directions progress was made, but the traditional divisions in Indian society still persisted.

The Indians of Canada also emerged onto the national political stage in the late 1960s. Canada's race relations have never exhibited the raw, brutal characteristics seen in the United States in the lynching of Negroes and the extermination of Indians. The Canadian philosophy has been to accept pluralism as a feature of national development. This philosophy began with the Two Canadas, English and French; yet, despite its greater tolerance, the philosophy incorporated the belief that English (and Scottish) norms were superior to all others. The Canadian Indians were penned into reservations, where they were known as Status Indians and were supervised by a paternalistic white administration. As in the United States, after a long period of population decline their numbers rose dramatically in the 1960s, and by 1970 there were approximately 250,000 Status Indians as well as about 260,000 others, known as *métis* being of mixed white – Indian descent. As in the United States, their conditions were poor, and unemployment among Indians ran at 50 per cent. Although forming 3 per cent of the total population, Indians form 30 per cent of the jail population: most being sentenced for petty crimes like drunkenness and vagrancy.

In 1967, two new representative organisations were founded: the National Indian Brotherhood for the people of the reservations and the Native Council of Canada for the *métis*. When Pierre Trudeau became Prime Minister he announced the goal of a 'just society'. The Indians began to demand a more equal share in development resources, and although they still received much less than other communities they made some progress.

A Canadian consciousness that there was a need to efface the image of an Anglo-dominated society was reflected in changes in immigration policy which to some extent anticipated those in the United States. The immigration regulations were modified in 1962, and in 1967 the previous overt bias towards Northern Europe was effaced by what was called the 'assessment' system of admission. The applicant was required to accumulate points, based on his education and training, his occupational skill, the occupational demand, arranged employment, etc. Nobody scoring less than 50 per cent was admitted. Because Canada had no requirement for unskilled workers (other than in service jobs: hotels, hospitals, etc.) the emphasis was upon professional, middle-class immigrants. However, Asians or Africans who met the Canadian standards could expect entry. Between 1968 and 1972, 52,000 persons arrived from the former British West Indies.[8] India also contributed towards the flow (about 20,000 admitted), while the victims of General Amin's expulsion of the Asians from Uganda were also accepted: about 6000, mainly the Aga Khan's followers, the Ismailis, who were energetic business and professional people.

Canada's action to improve its standing in the Third World was somewhat modified by the recession which followed the escalation of oil prices. In 1975, the Canadian government issued a Green Paper on immigration, which indicated that recent massive immigration had created problems of overcrowding; in Toronto, Montreal and Vancouver in particular. Canadian regulations were tightened up to prevent persons coming in as tourists and later claiming immigrant status. It seems probable that the new restrictions affected all immigrants, but (as in the United States) black and brown people deduced that the measures were aimed at them.

*

The concern manifested in North America for esteem in the Third World was expressed in Britain in the 1940s and 1950s, but thereafter the British mentally withdrew into their own island and rated the opinion of the outside world much less than the growing sentiment of exclusion voiced from within.

The 1950s were Britain's Commonwealth decade; they were also the last period in which the British economy expanded, and fulfilled its nineteenth century role of innovation. Certain industries—like the car industry—were then out in front, responding to world demands. Certain older industries—such as textiles and steel—still seemed important, and needed manpower. Britain's growing consumer demands, which included better transport and housing, needed to be satisfied. All these signs of apparent growth depended upon a supply of labour.

Britain continued to function as a country of emigration. Thousands of British girls – the war brides – left for Canada and the United States. A sustained flow of emigrants departed to Australia under the assisted passages scheme; the numbers emigrating rose from about 30,000 per annum to over 70,000 (the highest number of assisted British emigrants to Australia was 73,501 in 1965). The White Australia policy was still enforced, and only natives of the United Kingdom were accepted. When a would-be U.K. emigrant had a coloured wife he was unlikely to be taken, and black and brown applicants at Australia House in London were not considered. Australia preferred to recruit Greeks and Sicilians in preference to black British. The tide of British emigration to Australia only subsided when the Labour government of Gough Whitlam substantially reduced immigrant totals.

Down to the early 1970s, Britain's population was reduced more by emigration than it was augmented by immigration. The first great influx came in the late 1950s, when the West Indians (led by men who had served in the R.A.F. and British war industries) began to arrive by the shipload. Most came independently, but some were directly recruited from Britain. For nearly twenty years London Transport turned to Barbados to provide the crews for London's buses and underground trains, and at the peak over 5000 Barbadians were recruited annually. Similarly, the shortage of nurses in Britain's hospitals was filled by advertising for trained nurses in the Caribbean. (As Minister of Health 1960–3, Enoch Powell issued an appeal to West Indian nurses to come to Britain.)

There was a much smaller influx from South Asia in the 1950s. Most of the pioneers were Sikh ex-soldiers, or Muslims who had worked as sailors on British passenger ships plying to the Orient. The new arrivals congregated in the inner-city areas from which the more prosperous English workers were moving out. In general, they attracted little attention; though there were ugly exceptions, like the anti-immigrant riots in Nottingham and Notting Hill (London) in 1958. Unrestricted immigration from the Commonwealth was brought to an end by the Commonwealth Immigrants Act, 1962, passed by the Conservative government amid pious declarations that it was not intended as a bar against the entry of black and brown people. Henceforth, entry was controlled by 'work voucher', and the intention was to regulate numbers in relation to the demands of industry.

The Liberal and Labour parties in opposition in 1962 voted solidly against the new restrictions, yet when Labour came into office in 1964 in very little time the regulations were tightened drastically and entry was restricted to those workers which Britain most needed; some were semi-skilled (as for public transport) but increasingly the emphasis was upon professional immigrants, especially doctors. As a gesture towards the concept of multi-racialism, the Labour government also introduced a Race Relations Act in 1965. The Act was intended to counter racial discrimination, but its scope was limited and it was not backed by effective legal sanctions. The Act made incitement to racial hatred an offence, but the only prosecutions were initiated against attempts to introduce Black Power into Britain: the chief culprit being Michael X, a West Indian counterpart of Malcolm X.

The 1962 Act was intended to halt the 'flood', now being deplored by defenders of a white Britain, but thereafter the Asian immigration continued at a steady pace. The 1962 Act permitted the entry of the dependants of those already working in Britain, the Indians and Pakistanis were able to bring in large numbers of their countrymen as their children and relatives. Moreover, the restrictions did not apply to British passport holders, and increasingly Asians arrived via East Africa. The agreements which gave independence to Kenya, Tanzania, Uganda, Malawi and Zambia included as part of the over-all package a provision that the people originally from South Asia domiciled in those countries who did not opt for the citizenship of the new states might claim United Kingdom citizenship (see Map 2). Some of the East African Asians came from families domiciled in Africa for two generations or more; but many were recent arrivals.* As the number of arrivals from East Africa increased, the Labour government increasingly viewed the phenomenon as a 'problem' (though most of the people from East Africa, at this time, were able to set up a business, or enter a profession such as accountancy, after reaching Britain). In 1968 an unprecedented piece of legislation barred holders of British passports

---

* There was a category known as 'British Protected Persons' who did not come from what was previously British India (which made them British subjects), but who nevertheless travelled on British passports, though they came from territories outside British jurisdiction, such as Portuguese Goa. A large proportion of the Indians in East Africa belonged to this category, and by various devices they gained admission to Britain, but eventually the courts declared them ineligible for entry.

from entering Britain unless they actually 'belonged' to the United Kingdom. The East African Asians were allotted a 'D-passport' which allowed them to travel anywhere in the world – except to Britain. For the D-passport holders there was a quota of 5000 entry certificates per annum: they were told they must form a 'queue', for nothing fulfils the British conception of orderliness more than the spectacle of people queueing for some scarce commodity.

Once again, the Labour government tried to balance a policy of racial discrimination by a token gesture towards the multi-racial ideal. A second Race Relations Act, also introduced in 1968, was supposed to supplement the inadequate legislation of 1965. The main aim was to end discrimination in employment, but as the Act eschewed any tough sanctions against offenders its impact was still very limited. A Race Relations Board was set up, responsible for taking action against discrimination, and a Community Relations Commission created, responsible for promoting good relations in general, without any very clear mandate. The Board showed great reluctance to prosecute in cases of blatant discrimination, and when it did take action – on behalf of an Asian member of the Conservative Party, excluded from a local Conservative club – the courts refused to intervene.

When the Conservatives returned to office in 1970, they hastened to introduce legislation to make it even more difficult for Commonwealth citizens to enter Britain. The 'patrial' concept was introduced, which limited the right of entry to those whose own parents had been born in Britain. Powers against illegal immigrants were strengthened, and a vague provision was made for the repatriation of persons who asked to leave, or who were convicted of offences, or found suffering from mental illness. In reality, the 1971 Act made little difference, as the flow of worker-immigrants had already been stemmed (except for the entry of doctors and other skilled persons in scarce supply in Britain). It was still possible for dependants to join immigrants already in residence, though the entry process was made more difficult.

At the 1971 Census it was discovered that some 6 per cent of the population of England and Wales had been born outside the United Kingdom, compared with 3 per cent in 1961 (1971: 2,855,000; 1961: 1,420,000). However, 676,000 of this 2,855,000 were born in the Irish Republic and only 1,21,000 had come from the New Commonwealth countries. The concentration of immigrants in 1971 was greatest in the South-East (9·4 per cent of the total), while Greater London – within the South-East region – possessed an immigrant population accounting for 14·3 per cent of the total. The all-England average was 5·9 per cent and, outside the South-East, only the West Midlands (mainly the great conurbation of Birmingham) had an immigrant population above the national average (6·2 per cent). Wales and the North had received the smallest percentage of overseas people (2·1 and 1·6 per cent).

However, the Census figures do not properly record the numbers of those who the native British call 'immigrants'. Whereas in the United States an immigrant is one who was born outside the country (though the next generation, and many more may still be 'hyphenated' Americans – Italian-Americans, Afro-Americans, etc.), in British eyes all who have a skin-tone darker than that of the natives are regarded as immigrants.

The numbers registered by the 1971 Census as born in India, Pakistan and Bangladesh total 461,930. Yet the Census also reveals that out of this number there were 44,635 both of whose parents were born in Britain (some demographers call them 'white Indians') and these ought to be excluded from the 'coloured' total. However, the immigrants from India include many families in which both parents have been domiciled in Britain for many years. Their children, born in Britain, are calculated to number about 230,000. Because most Muslims (Pakistanis and Bangladeshis) arrived as single men and their wives joined them only after a long interval, their combined total of British-born children numbers only about 42,000. Then there are about 80,000 Asians born in East Africa who have settled in Britain, and a small number of people of Indian origin from the Caribbean and Mauritius. Taking all these figures together there are probably about 750,000 to 800,000 people in Britain who, if pressed to identify themselves, would say they are British Asians (or perhaps more precisely Sikhs, Gujaratis, Punjabis, etc.).

There are also about three-quarters of a million people described as West Indians or blacks in Britain: 60 per cent coming from Jamaica, and the rest mainly from Barbados, Trinidad and Guyana. The Cypriots number between 100,000 and 150,000, and are mainly Greek-Orthodox Cypriots: because of the troubled history of the island in recent times, numbers fluctuate greatly. Also from the Mediterranean are smaller numbers of Maltese. One of the smallest and least visible of the New Commonwealth communities is that of the Chinese: who come from Hong Kong and Singapore with a few from mainland China. Their numbers fluctuate, and many are temporary visitors; the total is about 70,000. None of these groups is as numerous as the Irish, numbering over one million.

The group which has made the greatest impact, both positively and negatively, is that from the Caribbean. West Indian cricketers, West Indian music (featuring steel bands and the reggae), West Indian writers (like George Lamming, Andrew Salkey and V. S. Naipaul) and West Indian theatre (notably the Dark and Light) are all integral parts of British culture. The Notting Hill Carnival, the great annual West Indian festival, is a major event for the people of West London. Most native Britons are aware that their hospitals and their buses just would not function without the West Indian contribution.

Yet British blacks are also among the most deprived and alienated of the non-white communities: there is a striking contrast between the relative contentment of most of those who came as immigrants and the resentment of those born in Britain. Many young blacks have gained little from British schools and about one-quarter of them are unemployed. Some drift into petty crime, and the arrival of mugging on the British scene is attributed to them. Black people appear to receive more than their share of attention from the police.[9] The British police have attracted no more than a handful of blacks into their ranks (in striking contrast to America), and their attitude to black people often displays ignorance and sometimes enmity. When arrested, many black people are roughed up in unexplained circumstances. Consequently, in an area of black settlement such as Brixton in South London, the relationship between black teenagers and policemen continually presses towards violence. In the summer of 1976 the Notting Hill Carnival was sadly marred by a pitched battle between black youths and the police.

The people from India – Sikhs and Gujaratis – come from communities which have long had a tradition of adventuring overseas.[10] They are resourceful and adaptable and socially mobile. The Sikhs retain a fierce attachment to their own religion, symbolised by the turban and the uncut beard. Arriving in Britain as yeoman farmers they go to work in factories, but they are determined that their sturdy sons (and daughters) shall be scientists, engineers, business managers. The Gujaratis mainly brought with them a pre-existing familiarity with trade and industry; they have set up their own firms, or have gone to work as tough industrial operatives. Wherever Indians have gone on strike for better conditions, there have been Gujarati organisers and leaders.

The Pakistanis are also mainly from a rural background; they come from the harsh districts of Punjab and the North-West Frontier. They are still a predominantly male community (1971: 98,040 males and

36,575 females), and many live in dormitories where conditions are crude. The Pakistanis are more completely concentrated in unskilled or semi-skilled jobs than the Indians. Their main social centre is the mosque, and they are not as domesticated or as well organised as the Indians. Down to 1971, the Muslims of East Bengal were also Pakistanis: thereafter they became Bangladeshis. Less tough than the Pakistanis of the North-West they are perhaps more remote from the main stream of British life than any other immigrant group. The native British learn to respect the Sikhs; they enjoy many aspects of West Indian culture, but they dislike what they know about those they call the 'Pakis' (actually the Bangladeshis). In the British equivalent of the white blacklash in America, these small, dark men from East Bengal have been the targets of vicious attacks – 'Paki-bashing', as it is called.

Among the other immigrant communities, the Greek Cypriots and the Chinese are concentrated in the catering business and there are few towns anywhere in Britain without a Chinese or Greek restaurant. Increasingly, the hotel business relies upon foreign labour from outside the Commonwealth. For there are boundary lines between foreign workers, as there are between the native British and the immigrants. The long hours and low pay which go with hotel employment mean that the New Commonwealth people avoid these jobs. Those who work as dishwashers, porters, maids and waiters are mainly Spaniards, Portuguese, and people from North Africa. These are the real *lumpenproletariat*. These provide the migrant workers of Western Europe.

Britain still retains the image of the newcomer as *immigrant*. Apart from the National Front and other right-wing groups, which call for the compulsory repatriation of coloured people, all sections of British opinion accept that when people are admitted to Britain they have the right to stay: even though they may not be regarded as deserving full equality of status with the natives.* In Western Europe, the foreign workers have no such expectation of becoming permanent residents: Germany has invented the term *Gastarbeiter*, 'guest worker', to describe the grim reality that outsiders are wanted to meet the labour shortage but are wanted as work-units only; they are not expected to settle and make homes for their families.

* This is very evident in housing policy. Over a quarter of the homes in Britain (27·6%) are in the public housing sector. The local authorities who control public housing insist that all applicants must qualify by residing *within the area* for five years before they can be granted accommodation. Thus only 11 per cent of the Indians and 6 per cent of the Pakistanis have been allotted local authority housing.

*

It is estimated that in the mid-1970s there are 15 million foreign workers in Western Europe. Switzerland, with a total population of 6·3 million, has one million foreigners; making 17 per cent of the population and over 25 per cent of the workforce. France and West Germany both have over 4 million foreigners in their midst. In the first decade after the Second World War, the rapidly expanding industries of Northern Europe drew recruits from nearby. West German industry expanded by employing refugees from East Germany; French industry recruited workers from the peasants of the countryside, as British industry did over one hundred years earlier. When these sources proved inadequate, workers from the impoverished south of Italy were drawn in. Finally, as the German 'economic miracle' was followed by similar expansion in France and Benelux, Western Europe turned to the Third World for labour.

Just as Britain drew upon its former colonies to work in the *métropole*, so the Europeans exploited their imperial legacy for post-imperial development. France had a ready supply of labour in the territories formerly administered in North Africa: Algeria, Morocco and Tunisia (see Map 2). Germany could not so easily turn to former colonies for Germany's empire had disappeared over fifty years before. Yet Germany had always nourished a special paternal relationship with Turkey. Kaiser Wilhelm had promoted the Berlin to Baghdad railway to bring the Ottoman Empire into Germany's orbit, and the alliance of 1914–18 had been sustained even after Germany's defeat. The 'syphoning' effect of these imperial legacies can be understood from the actual figures for worker migration.

Immigrants from North Africa and Turkey to France and Germany
(1971 estimate)

From		To France	To Germany
	Algeria	754,462	1,985
	Morocco	194,296	10,921
	Tunisia	106,845	9,918
	Turkey	18,325	653,000

The 'magnetic' attraction whereby the two countries draw in two entirely different streams of workers is very striking. In addition,

Germany obtained recruits from the 'lesser breeds' of south-east Europe, hiring thousands of Greeks and Yugoslavs.

Germany has the largest number of foreign workers among E.E.C. members, and during the 1960s imported ten times as many as Britain. The *Gastarbeiters* are regarded as just that: temporary workers allowed in upon sufferance. The German strategy is to increase the flow during boom periods and to turn off the tap whenever trade is slack. Yet Germany's temporary visitors are trying to behave just like immigrants, as in Britain or any other 'host' country. They fetch their families and try to settle. It has been found that there are 400,000 foreign (mainly Turkish) children of school-going age in West Germany, of whom 250,000 are not in school. Many are illegally working. German policy is to put the foreigners into barracks controlled by the employing firms, and only slowly are they moving into rented accommodation. German government policy is against the recruitment of any brown or black people: 'It is an internal directive of the government.'[11] Nevertheless German public opinion has manifested anti-immigration tendencies. An opinion poll taken in 1975 revealed that 50 per cent of Germans believed that their economic difficulties were caused by the foreign workers, and the Federal Minister for Economic Development announced in January 1975 that the government wanted half a million of them to return home. The *Gastarbeiters* did not heed this warning, for they know that German industry in the 1970s cannot function efficiently without them.

France has a long tradition of taking in foreign workers – in part to compensate for the missing manpower caused by casualties in a succession of wars – but only in the 1950s and 1960s were the bulk of them black and brown. France has swallowed a high proportion of illegal immigrants, smuggled across the frontiers, but their presence was accepted by the administration. Lacking any rights, they cannot make any demands on the social services and they are compelled to work for low rates of pay. Shanty towns, *bidonvilles*, made of discarded trash materials grew up around Paris, Marseilles and Lyons. They became a public scandal and many were torn down, but their inhabitants dispersed into *microbidonvilles*. This made it easier for the native French to ignore them, and the only groups interested in securing any human rights for the illegal immigrants are some Maoists and some radical Christians: the powerful communist trade unions ignore them, in their strategy of trying to win over the respectable workers and the bourgeoisie. Nobody protests when the police make raids and expel illegal immigrants with no appeal. (From 1964 to 1974 it was possible for those without work permits to regularise their situation. This regularisation was stopped completely in 1974.)

*

The Netherlands has a justifiable reputation for mobilising its social services to meet the special needs of immigrants, and when in the 1950s thousands of Eurasian Dutch citizens were suddenly expelled by Indonesia there was a national programme to integrate them within Dutch society.[12] When ten years later, large numbers of Dutch colonial subjects arrived for settlement from Surinam (the territory next to Guyana) they were accepted, and nobody suggested exclusion in the manner in which Britain had banned the entry of Commonwealth citizens and U.K. passport holders. By 1975, when Surinam was about to obtain independence, there were about 120,000 settlers from Surinam in the Netherlands. Government policy was not changed, but the attitude of the native Dutch hardened appreciably. There were anti-Surinamese riots in The Hague and in Amsterdam (where 6 per cent of the population is black), and while still accepting responsibility for its colonial citizens the Dutch government issued a policy paper calling for the stabilisation of the immigrant population at existing numbers.

*

Throughout Europe, the issue of immigration is suspended, between the opposed pressures of economic reality and political wishful thinking. Many Europeans desire to get back to a former age, when everything was less complicated; and to them the newcomers are a symbol of a new world which they cannot understand and do not wish to understand. Without doubt, yearnings after vanished imperial glories play a big part in this craving for things as they once were.

Dislike of the immigrants has been expressed in direct attacks upon individuals or little groups. The Algerians in France continue to be a special target (in 1973, six were murdered in one month in Marseilles alone). Immigrants are subjected to boycotts and other social and economic pressures. Fringe political parties make them a target: in France there is the *Ordre Nouveau*, and in Switzerland the movement to restrict immigration by appeal to a popular referendum, led by

Schwarzenberg. There is much talk of *Überfremdung* or 'excessive foreign-ness' as threatening domination of the country by outsiders.

The immigrants have made almost no attempt to fight back against discrimination – social, political or economic. Even where their numbers are relatively substantial, they exist in a condition of powerlessness. Only a tiny minority talk of challenging Western Europe by taking up the weapons of the urban guerrilla. Some hope that the Third World may come to their aid, but in so many cases the Third World countries remain the clients of the West. The powerlessness of black and brown people, as individuals, is mirrored in their powerlessness as nations. However, they are not prepared to accept this condition forever. The Third World is stirring angrily and restlessly. There are a number of ways whereby this powerlessness may be ended. 'Betting on the Many' comes into them all. One important road which is open to them is that of the United Nations. This, above all, seems to be the road to the future.

6 Strategies of Third World Advance

IN the first enthusiasm of independence the new nations believed that a new world had dawned. In almost every case (apart from Vietnam and Algeria) the Western colonial powers surrendered their authority with much greater alacrity than anyone had expected. Would they not, therefore, be induced to relinquish their grip upon the international system in the same way? The new nations marshalled themselves together, believing that in solidarity lay their strength. Only slowly did they come to realise that the walls of the city would not fall at the first blast of the trumpet. The West still maintained what were regarded as imperial outposts, strongholds, deep inside the territory of the Third World. These were identified as South Africa, with its remaining white bastions, Rhodesia and the Portuguese colonies, and Israel with (in undefined fashion) Lebanon and Jordan. South Africa was identified as the enemy from the start; only gradually did Israel assume the same character in the eyes of the entire Third World. These symbolic 'white colonies' attracted more attention than the remaining real colonies, though several of these did come under fierce scrutiny by the U.N. Trusteeship Council.

The first efforts at Third World solidarity were somewhat tentative and experimental. In 1945 the Arab League came into being; the first of the regional organisations having the purpose of establishing a sense of solidarity and liberation from Western imperial overlordship. The original members, who formed the League of Arab States in March 1945, were Egypt, Iraq, Syria, Lebanon, Jordan, Saudi Arabia and Yemen: together with a representative of the Palestinian Arabs. Even at this early stage the principle was enunciated that a people under colonial rule (as Palestine was still) should be considered as equal to recognised states if they formed a nation or an ethnic or racial family. The Arab League was subsequently joined by Libya, Morocco, Sudan and Tunis. Very rapidly, the members of the Arab League focused their activities upon the Jewish effort to consolidate and expand the new state

of Israel. All the Arab League members combined to send in their
armies to liquidate Israel; a state of war commenced, which was to
persist – through different phases of hot and cold war – for the next
thirty years. About 900,000 Palestinian Arabs had to flee from their
homes (subsequently, 1948–70, about 600,000 Jews fled from the lands
of the Arab League into Israel).

The reaction of the new United Nations to the Arab attacks was
strongly condemnatory. The Soviet representative at the U.N., Andrei
Gromyko, observed: 'The states whose forces have invaded Palestine
have ignored the Security Council's resolution. . . . It is not in the
interest of the United Nations in general, or of the Security Council in
particular, to tolerate such a situation, where decisions of the Council
designed to put an end to warfare are being flouted.' Early in 1949 U.N.
mediation succeeded in bringing about ceasefire arrangements with all
the Arab states. But this resolved nothing, for the Arab League insisted
that any settlement must include the return of the Palestinian refugees
to their old homes.

The Arab League owed its strength and substance to a shared feeling
of hostility to Israel and to what was identified as World Zionism. In
August 1948, the government of Iraq (then conservative and pro-
Western) declared Zionism to be a crime, along with Nazism and
communism: a foretaste of things to come.

The other moves towards Third World solidarity were based upon
vaguer, ideological, bonds and were much less powerful. An Asian
Relations Conference was convened at New Delhi in March 1947, and
invitations were sent to the Hebrew University, Jerusalem, as well as to
Arab institutions and to representatives from China and South-east
Asia. No invitations went out to Africans, though two South African
Indian leaders attended. The subjects considered included racial
problems, inter-Asian migration, industrialisation and labour. A
proposal for a permanent organisation to be housed at Delhi was put
forward by Nehru, but this elicited no response. Many of the delegates
(especially those from South-east Asia) suspected that there was an
element of Indian imperialism behind it all.

An Asian Socialist Conference was convened at Rangoon in January
1953. This was by no means restricted to Asian participants. Once
again, Israel was invited to attend, while 'fraternal observers' from
Europe included Clement Attlee from Britain and Milovan Djilas from
Yugoslavia. The conference set up a small permanent body, and
subsequently an Anti-Colonial Bureau was constituted to make contact

with anti-colonial movements in Africa, still largely unknown to the Asians.

The Rangoon conference was never credited with the importance which was attributed to the Asian – African Conference convened at Bandung in Indonesia in April 1955. Although the conference has been identified with the Afro-Asian movement, of the twenty-nine nations who assembled at Bandung only three (Liberia, Ethiopia and Ghana) were from Black Africa and no African leader made any mark upon the proceedings.[1] (In 1955 Ghana was still the Gold Coast, a British colony.)

Bandung was marked by a conscious spirit of solidarity among nations newly freed from Western rule. Nobody was more conscious of the symbolism of the occasion than the host, President Sukarno, who saw events and trends in apocalyptic terms, coining the magic words OLDEFO (old-established forces) for the white imperial powers, led both by the United States and the Soviet Union, and NEFO (new emerging forces) for the non-white world, led by China, and united in their experience of white dominance. Opening the conference, Sukarno claimed: 'This is the first inter-continental conference of coloured peoples in the history of mankind.'

Not all the delegates were as concerned to emphasise that their unity was based upon their being brown and black people. Nehru pressed for an invitation to be sent to the Soviet Union; a move emphatically opposed by Kotelawala of Ceylon and others. Yet, in his desire to emphasise the importance of non-alignment, Nehru used words which could be interpreted as expressing a condemnation of the continuance of white dominance. He declared: 'It is an intolerable thought to me that the great countries of Asia and Africa should have come out of bondage into freedom only to degrade themselves. . . . I will not tie myself to this degradation . . . and become a camp-follower of others.'

Certain speakers were even more specific in declaring that Bandung marked a break with the old world of white dominance. President Carlos Romulo of the Philippines – not a politician noted for radical sentiments – made racial equality the main theme of his speech:

There has not been, and there is not, a Western colonial regime which has not imposed to a greater or lesser degree on the people it ruled a doctrine of their own racial inferiority. We have known, and some of us still know, the searing experience of being demeaned in our own lands, of being systematically relegated to subject status, not only politically and economically and militarily – but racially as well. . . . To bolster his rule, to justify his own power to himself, Western white man assumed that his superiority lay in his very genes, in the colour of his skin. This made the lowest drunken sot superior in colonial society to the highest product of culture and scholarship and industry among the subject people.

President Romulo warned the Bandung audience against being caught themselves in 'the racist trap'. He insisted that for Asians:

the deepest source of our own confidence in ourselves had come from the deeply-rooted knowledge that the white man was wrong, that in proclaiming the superiority of his race, *qua* race, he stamped himself with his own weakness. . . . If we respond to the white man's prejudices against us as non-whites with prejudices against whites simply because they are white. . . . This would in the deepest sense mean giving up all hope of human freedom in our time.

In its final communiqué, the conference made a number of references to racialism. One 'condemned racialism as a means of cultural suppression', while another committed the signatories to 'eradicate every trace of racialism that might exist in their own countries'. The communiqué closed with a declaration affirming the equality of all races. Thus Bandung was not intended as a stage for the expression of non-white or anti-white solidarity, and the way ahead was viewed as linked with the extension of equality and non-alignment. The way ahead was to prove unprofitable; for the gatherings after Bandung – conferences convened at Belgrade (1961), Cairo (1964), Algiers (1965) and Havana (1966) – all revealed the chronic differences which frustrated the Afro-Asian movement. These differences were partly ideological but also partly temperamental. As one involved observer reported: 'The Asians find the Africans jejune and overemotional and the Africans find the Asians hidebound and patronising.'[2] However, in August 1976, the non-aligned movement received renewed impetus from the savage repression by white South Africa of the peoples of the black townships, which united all the participants at the summit meeting in Sri Lanka in demands for tougher sanctions against South Africa.

As the African countries burst out of colonial control they increasingly asserted their own special African identity. Kwame Nkrumah was among the first of the top-rank leaders to declare that the new nations must find themselves not within the artificial boundaries bequeathed by the departed colonialists but in a new coming together, a rally of peoples having a common African inheritance. Attempts to express this 'togetherness' by means of political merger, in new federations or confederations had no success however, and after some brief trials the former British and French colonies acquiesced in the boundary-lines of statehood they had inherited from their European overlords. Even the mini-state of the Gambia was unable to reach an agreement with Senegal which embraced the river-state on all sides: though both the ex-British and ex-French peoples concerned had a common tribal and linguistic inheritance, all being Wolofs (see Map 2).

African unity developed partly on symbolic or mystical lines. The ancient kingdoms of West Africa were regarded as the cradle of an advanced African civilisation. Cheikh Anta Diop, the Senegalese writer, states that Black Africa had been 'The first to invent mathematics, astronomy, the calendar, sciences in general, the arts, religion, agriculture, social organisation, medicine, writing, technical skills and architecture.'[3] The Wolofs joined the many other candidates (Irish, Norse, etc.) for the claim of discovering America. A philosophy embodying the African view of life emerged in the concept of *négritude*, first enunciated by Léopold Senghor of Senegal.

A wider concept of black internationalism was envisaged by writers across the Atlantic. For many American and West Indian blacks, Africa remained the mother, though long separated from her children.* Among Caribbean writers and leaders who fostered the idea, Marcus Garvey from Jamaica (1887–1940) was the first and perhaps the most important. Other Caribbean thinkers of international importance, such as George Padmore and C. L. R. James of Trinidad, and Frantz Fanon of Martinique, stressed the struggle against colonial exploitation, rather than the African identity, though the younger, more radical writers, especially Stokely Carmichael, have merged their African and revolutionary identities.

Among the rulers of Africa, a certain scepticism emerged concerning the Pan-African movement. More emphasis is placed upon the Organisation of African Unity (O.A.U.), founded in 1963, which convenes meetings of all the heads of state each year and attempts to determine a common policy upon major continental issues. The O.A.U. views Africa as a territorial rather than an ideological unity, and the non-black Arab states of the north, together with predominantly Indian Mauritius, are accepted as full members.

* Brazil went through a liberal period in the 1950s when, under President Kubitschek, an effort was made to stress the links between Brazil and West Africa ('Operation Panamerica'). Little survived under subsequent military regimes, except certain cultural institutions centred on Bahia, the old slave-city.

Encompassing the Afro-Asian movement and the Pan-African movement there is the Third World revolutionary movement, sometimes called the tri-continental movement, whose undisputed head is China, though its most active promoter is Cuba. An acknowledgement of its philosophy was given in 1963 by the Pan-Africanist Nkrumah when he declared: 'We are fighting not against race, creed or colour. We are fighting against an economic system which is designed to exploit us and keep us in a state of permanent subjection.'[4] Those to whom 'Betting on the Many' represents the wave of the future responded to this message of revolution.

The West, so defensive on its own doorstep, expected to maintain a place in the Third World by a judicious policy of distributing economic aid and specialist technical advice, with the dual object of perpetuating the economic and financial ties of former colonial times and also of retaining markets for Western products. The United States was by far the largest operator of aid programmes, demonstrating that combination of idealism and commercial self-interest which has traditionally shaped American foreign policy. Aid flourished in the 1950s and early 1960s, but almost everywhere there was a signal failure to stimulate that 'take-off into sustained growth' which American economists had forecast. Countries like India became burdened with billions of dollars of debt, which in some cases required repayments to the donor which were larger than his current instalments of aid. Instead of a spirit of gratitude marking the relationship, the recipients of aid increasingly demonstrated feelings of resentment that they had been saddled with such ominous obligations and had obtained such minimal benefits. On the donor side, there was equally a feeling of disillusionment as it became obvious that the recipients increasingly required more, not less, support. The American aid programme was tapered off, and the other donors of the 'group of ten' also cut back their assistance.

The failure of the West's aid strategy brought different kinds of response. Some Third World countries merely called for more. A few countries attempted to evolve alternative approaches to development based upon their own social and economic realities. This meant shifting from development based upon industrialisation and capital investment to rural development based upon mobilising the resources of the people. The outstanding examples of this rural, agricultural strategy were the People's Republics of China and North Vietnam, though Burma also imitated a similar policy in 'the Burmese way to socialism' and President Nyerere of Tanzania led his people along the same way, following the Urusha Declaration.

For a time it appeared as though Israel might make a unique contribution to Third World development by training people in Asia and Africa in techniques based upon acquired human skills rather than upon high technology and heavy investment. Israeli technicians helped to make friends for the beleaguered little country, and promoted a countervailing influence to Arab claims for Afro-Asian solidarity. Unwisely, the Israelis also embarked upon programmes of military training and arms supply to a number of Third World countries, from Singapore to Uganda. This form of aid suggested more of an imperialistic mission, and when Israel was involved in a third and fourth campaign against the Arab armies (in 1967 and 1973) her erstwhile friends in the Third World turned overnight into hostile critics.

For many years, both on the Arab and on the Jewish side, it was contended that the conflict was not racial in character: some argued that both sides belonged to the same Semitic family, both as regards race and religion. Yet, increasingly, racial overtones predominated in the long-fought duel, though the racial element was ideological rather than physical. Zionism was depicted as the latest version of Western dominance, previously manifested as imperialism and Nazism. The Palestinian Arabs were seen as the true sons of the soil, symbolising the dispossessed, the disinherited peoples of the earth. The contrast was reinforced by Israeli military successes in three wars, which were seen by the Arab victims as evidence of a race mastery combined with a superiority in weaponry giving an uncannily unfair advantage over the sons of the soil.

The unequal duel was dramatically changed, and to some extent reversed, after the fourth war by two new developments. One was the realisation by the oil producers that they controlled *the* ultimate economic weapon. The other was the discovery by Arab guerrillas that they also had a weapon which could strike terror into the hearts of their enemies.

In Britain's long, rearguard action against economic decline, a major role must be accorded to those British advisers to the sheikhs of the oil states in the Persian Gulf, who for more than twenty years persuaded the rulers that they must not try to raise the price of oil too high! Only after the formation of opec (the Organisation of Petroleum Exporting Countries), and as an almost blind gesture of protest against Israeli expansion did the oil states hike up the price: to discover, to their astonishment, that the Western world had tamely to accept their demands. Led by Libya and other more radical regimes, the OPEC group changed all the rules of the game. At last, the economic dominance of the West had been challenged and overthrown.

The guerrillas also made their breakthrough with the discovery that the most effective pressure could be exerted not by striking directly at Israel, but at those who stood behind Israel. The Arab guerrillas, the *fedayin* ('martyrs'), had been on the attack since 1948 (and indeed for many years before), but their efforts had achieved little or nothing. Whenever the guerrillas struck at an Israeli outpost or settlement their enemies struck back twice as hard. If the guerrillas were traced to an Arab house, then that house was razed to the ground. The relatives of known guerrillas were placed under the most severe restrictions, and were frequently deported. Any raiders actually captured would say farewell to freedom. Thus, for twenty years, *fedayin* attempts to terrorise the Israeli border areas were a failure.

Then, quite suddenly, the guerrillas changed their tactics and turned their attention to the friends and supporters of Israel. Their first major success was the hijacking of passenger aircraft. They discovered that an airline captain with a planeload of passengers was totally helpless. There followed the spectacular kidnapping of British and American aircraft, followed in several cases by their destruction. Gradually, the world's airlines evolved measures to neutralise the hijackers – though nothing could ever completely rule out the possibility. Then the guerrillas turned to concealing bombs upon aircraft and even to attacking them upon the ground. From these yet more violent techniques they went on to occupy embassies and other highly sensitive buildings, holding important people at gunpoint until their demands were met. These methods, which made no impression upon the tough Israeli authorities, were very successful against the 'soft' governments of Western Europe.

It was significant that techniques invented by the Arab guerrillas were rapidly imitated by militant groups claiming to represent other deprived and disinherited communities, such as the I.R.A. (Irish Republican Army), the Black Panthers, and the urban guerrillas of Latin America. These attacks were not enough to bring about lasting victories, but they achieved important propaganda successes. Previously, public opinion in the United States and in Europe had been overwhelmingly on the side of Israel (in part because of feelings of guilt about Nazi genocide: feelings subtly exploited by Israel). Like Belgium in the First World War, 'gallant little Israel' had been applauded for standing up to the Arab bullies. The Arab guerrillas succeeded in making the West feel that Israel was really rather a nuisance; that if only Israel would be a little more reasonable, life for everyone would be less complicated and less perilous. After the oil price-hike and the hijackings many in the Western world began to wish that Israel had never been invented.

One aspect of the guerrillas' terrorist campaign was that some previously regarded as extremists suddenly looked quite moderate. Perhaps in the hope that the Palestine Liberation Organisation can control the terrorists, the P.L.O. have rapidly been accorded legitimacy by France and other Western countries, and in November 1974 their leader, Yasser Arafat, was invited to address the United Nations. He stood at the rostrum still wearing desert head-dress, with a revolver at his belt.

The U.N. which welcomed Yasser Arafat was, to be sure, the largely Afro-Asian U.N. of later days and not the organisation dominated by the 'Big Five' (U.S.A., U.S.S.R., Britain, France, China) in the beginning. The transformation came in the early 1960s. We noted that, at the start, the U.N. contained only twelve states which could be called Afro-Asian, mainly belonging to the Middle East. Ten years later there were 25 Afro-Asians compared to 51 other states which might be labelled white. In 1961 there were still 51 white states, but the Afro-Asians totalled 53. The most spectacular change was the increase of the African states, rising from 3 per cent to 20 per cent of the total membership.

From the beginning, the U.N. was divided between two competing blocs, the Western and the Communist. The emergence of a third force was associated with the gradual build-up of an Afro-Asian group. Their first attempt to combine came at the time of the Korean war when, largely at Nehru's initiative, the representatives of the uncommitted Third World nations began to meet together at the U.N. So tenuous was the group that neither Ethiopia nor Liberia (the oldest African U.N. members) participated. However, the group used its voting strength increasingly on what appeared to be imperial issues, and by 1962 there were 55 states meeting regularly to co-ordinate policies. Of these 32 were African, 22 were Asian, 1 (Cyprus) was in the Middle-East orbit.

In 1960, on the initiative of forty-three Afro-Asian states, the General Assembly adopted a resolution on the granting of independence to colonial countries and peoples, requiring the colonial powers to hand over charge immediately. It was symptomatic of the changing character of the U.N. that the resolution received eighty-nine votes in favour, with none against, though nine Western countries decided to abstain (Australia, Belgium, Britain, Dominica, France, Portugal, South Africa, Spain and the United States). It was soon after this resolution that the dismantling of the British Empire ceased to be a measured, deliberate process and became a rush job.

Just as the Western bloc frequently dissolves over particular issues, the Afro-Asian group is not monolithic. The Arabs almost always act together, but other Africans and Asians do not always go along with them or with each other. What can be asserted with some certainty is that the group tends to coalesce whenever the United States or Britain is under fire for imperialistic activity. A former President of the General Assembly, Charles Malik of Lebanon, has concluded: 'Western causes have no chance of enlisting a majority in the U.N. today; and the principal defence that such causes can count on is the enjoyment of the right of veto by three Western powers in the Security Council and the fact that the decisions of the General Assembly have a juridical value only of recommendation.'[5]

The West is not only caught upon the defensive when central Western policies are challenged, but also when an issue marginal to the West comes under attack. In such cases, the Western members of the U.N. may prefer to bow to the inevitable Afro-Asian majority, or even try to court Third World favour by voting with the majority. The outstanding example of how the West has shifted its ground is provided by the long attempt within the U.N. to brand the white rulers of South Africa as pariahs.

When the U.N. was first established in 1945, the preamble to its Charter was written by Field-Marshal Smuts, then Prime Minister of South Africa and much respected as one of the principal architects of the former League of Nations. Yet, by the end of the first year of the U.N.'s existence, South Africa was under fire. The main indictment was brought by India, for recent legislation (termed 'the Ghetto Act') had placed the Indian population in South Africa under penalties restricting their right to trade and to live in white areas. Smuts replied to India's complaint by arguing that the matter was one of internal concern only (this was to be the standard South African defence against all U.N. indictments). In the debate which followed, Britain strongly upheld South Africa's case, as did the other White Commonwealth representatives: for very recently they had all been comrades in arms. The Communist countries solidly supported India, and the soon-to-be-familiar pattern of cold-war confrontation took shape. Adjudged an important issue, the Indian complaint required a two-thirds majority to pass. When the final vote was counted, 32 nations voted for India and 15 voted for South Africa, so that the resolution was carried.[6] Voting with the majority was the Communist bloc (6), the Afro-Asians (12), some Latin Americans (11), and 3 West European states. Voting with South Africa, there were Britain and the White Commonwealth (4), the United States and its Latin-American satellites (7), and the traditional friends of South Africa in Europe: Holland, Belgium, Luxemburg and Greece. Smuts told South African audiences that the U.N. was dominated by the coloured peoples. In 1947, the statement was palpably exaggerated; yet Smuts was only anticipating what was soon to come.

At the same time, the U.N. set up a Trusteeship Council to assume responsibility for all the former League mandates. Unlike the old system, the U.N. was given real power to intervene (much to the chagrin of British colonial administrators). All the former mandates were assigned by the supervising powers to the U.N. as trust territories, except for South West Africa, administered by South Africa, which Smuts claimed should now accede to the Union (see Map 2). The U.N. rejected the South African demand by thirty-seven votes to nil. None of the Western countries actually backed South Africa (for they were transferring their own mandates without delay) but nine states, led by Britain and the United States, abstained over the question.

Subsequently, both questions – the treatment of non-whites in South Africa itself, and the status of South West Africa – were brought before the U.N. time after time. The Western friends of South Africa soon deemed it expedient not to identify themselves openly with unpopular racial policies. As early as 1949, the United States shifted its position over the question of the South African Indians, and voted alongside India with the majority. The White Commonwealth abstained, and South Africa's only remaining open allies were Argentina, Brazil, Greece and the Netherlands.[7] When later, in 1949, a Franco-Mexican resolution called upon South Africa to meet India and Pakistan at a round-table conference, this was adopted by 47 votes with 12 abstentions, and only South Africa's own representative voted against. The years of total isolation had begun.

Nevertheless, the force of world public opinion was not enough to induce South Africa to modify its policies designed to create apartheid between whites and non-whites. The history of the U.N. is predominantly one of symbolic activity: only the most convinced believer in institutions of progress would have expected otherwise. The U.N. does control important actual resources through its agencies. The Third World gradually modified its strategy to try to exploit this angle.

Hence, the case of South West Africa was taken to the International Court at the Hague, though without any conclusive result, and eventually in October 1966 the U.N. General Assembly passed a resolution declaring that South Africa's mandate was terminated and the territory would thenceforward come directly under U.N. control. The resolution was passed by 114 votes to 2: the negative votes were those of South Africa and Portugal, but additionally 3 states abstained (Britain, France and Malawi). As before, South Africa ignored the verdict of the United Nations, and Britain with important mining interests in South West Africa also put aside its obligation to support the U.N.[8]

Frustrated in their direct attack upon South African racist policies, the Third World members of the U.N. have at any rate been able to deny to South Africa a place in many of the international institutions which come within the U.N.'s aegis. In seeking to understand how the United Nations has come to embody the conflict or confrontation between the white nations (sometimes referred to as 'the North') and the black and brown nations ('the South'), we ought to analyse the different roles of these international agencies in some detail.

Broadly speaking, one kind of agency represents the financial and technological interests of the white, advanced nations, and another kind attempts to mobilise resources on behalf of the black and brown poorer nations.[9] The Western countries also participate, with greater or less enthusiasm, within the second group: but because of its refusal to relinquish racist policies South Africa has been compelled to withdraw from all the organisations in this group.

The most important organisation of 'the North' is the International Monetary Fund, established in 1944. This is an international body for the provision of banking and credit on orthodox capitalist lines. Its permanent staff is drawn mainly from white countries: out of the total of 54 experts, 32 are Anglo (23 being Americans), 9 are from Western Europe, 7 are Asian, 2 are African, 2 come from Latin America. South Africa is a member of the I.M.F., but most Third World countries have stayed outside, as has the Soviet Union. The first major achievement of the I.M.F. was the General Agreement on Tariffs and Trade (GATT) which attempted to make the world safe for business interests.

Another Western-orientated body is the International Atomic

Energy Agency, founded in 1957 on American initiative. South Africa is a member of the I.A.E.A., being a major producer of uranium. The African states have tried to obtain greater representation on this body which is seen as a key factor for world peace or war; they have also tried to terminate South Africa's membership, but the United States has refused to accept a move which might adversely affect the supply of the material for nuclear energy.

The Third World majority within the U.N. has used its voting strength to change policies in several organisations, but though 'the Many' have the numbers 'the Strong' have the dollars. The Third World can make demands; but the U.N. relies heavily for the upkeep of its organisations upon the massive contributions of the United States, the Soviet Union, and the industrial nations of the West. By too obviously demonstrating that an organisation is expected to respond to their demands, the Third World may ensure that the United States is less than enthusiastic about underwriting the financial implications.

The oldest of the U.N. organisations is the International Labour Organisation (I.L.O.), first set up by the League in 1919. During the most intensive phase of the cold war, from about 1948–54, international trade-union politics was one of the principal battlegrounds between Moscow and Washington. The I.L.O. was then largely under Western influence, and the U.S.S.R. with its Communist satellites did not join the organisation until 1954. From 1960 African membership was increasingly important: with deeprooted memories of types of forced labour akin to slavery under various white regimes. Attacks upon Portuguese rule in Africa, upon White Rhodesia, and upon the pass laws of South Africa became ever more vigorous. In the end, the Africans forced South Africa to withdraw from the I.L.O. There was little protest by American or European delegates who doubtless wished to avoid guilt by association. In 1975 the Arab states successfully obtained 'observer status' for the P.L.O. within the I.L.O. This appeared to be the first move towards expelling Israel from the Organisation, but the United States (which contributes one-quarter of the I.L.O.'s budget) made it clear that this would entail American withdrawal also.

Another important vehicle for the Many was the World Health Organisation, established in 1946. This became a forum for cold-war encounters, and in 1949 the Soviet Union and its following left the W.H.O., to return only in 1957–8. Once again, the arrival of the Africans made a significant difference. In 1965, the World Health

Assembly voted to suspend and ultimately expel any member who is 'deliberately practising a policy of racial discrimination'. Seeing the warning signal, South Africa prudently left the W.H.O. The World Health Assembly also denounced the incidence of epidemics in South Vietnam consequent upon the American military presence there, and went on to criticise health conditions among Palestinian refugees in the Israeli-occupied territories. This criticism was jointly tabled by the United Arab Republic, Iraq, and the Soviet Union.

UNESCO, the United Nations Educational, Scientific and Cultural Organisation was also founded in 1946, and was also subject to Soviet arrivals and departures before the Africans entered *en masse* in 1960. South Africa quit UNESCO under pressure in 1965, following attacks upon discrimination in its system of education.[10] UNESCO has always included substantial Third World representation, both among its senior staff and also on its executive board. India has played a leading role from the beginning, and Egypt has also been important. The People's Republic of China was admitted in 1971 on entering the United Nations.

Having disposed of South Africa, UNESCO turned its attention to Israel, and after their occupation of old Jerusalem the Israelis proved very vulnerable to attack. Archaeological excavation is a major activity in Israel, and the methods they employ – involving what is considered to be the insensitive destruction of buildings and artifacts belonging to post-Judaic times – have often been condemned by non-Israeli archaeologists. In consequence, Israel was warned and then suspended from UNESCO in 1975 for what was described as a policy of vandalism in destroying Muslim and Christian monuments.

The last important U.N. organisation to become a symbol of the divide between 'North' and 'South' is UNCTAD, the U.N. Conference on Trade and Development, first brought together in 1964 on the initiative of the Third World and the Soviet Union. UNCTAD is often identified with the seventy-seven U.N. members who form the 'developing' (that is, poor) world. A great deal of its driving-power was provided by its first director, Anton Prebitsch of Brazil, and at different times the representatives of India, Nigeria, the Philippines, Yugoslavia and Chile have played leading parts.

Successive UNCTAD conferences have been attended by delegates from over-developed countries as well as the representatives of the 'group of seventy-seven'. Much was expected from UNCTAD II, the conference at Delhi in 1968, when strenuous efforts were made to get the group of ten, and other affluent countries, to give a definite commitment to allocate higher percentages of their G.N.P. to aid and investment in the Third World. The Delhi conference was, by general agreement, a dismal failure.

One of the by-products of Delhi was that, on the initiative of Algeria and Uganda, South Africa was expelled from the organisation, while Israel was conspicuously cold-shouldered by the seventy-seven. At Delhi also, as a by-product of superpower *détente*, an alliance developed between the U.S.A. and the U.S.S.R. in resisting Third World demands: 'Both camps showed a growing disillusion with the short-term political importance and development prospects of the Third World.'[11]

When UNCTAD IV convened at Nairobi in 1976, the poor nations were still conscious of the breakthrough achieved by OPEC in raising world commodity prices, and made far-reaching proposals to achieve world price agreements for raw materials. Though resisted strenuously by the affluent, consuming nations these were pressed hard by the producers. The polarisation of rich and poor, white and non-white, deplored at Bandung, seemed to be near.

What might have appeared to be a milestone on the road to racial equality was reached in 1965 with the sponsorship by the U.N. of the International Convention on the Elimination of all Forms of Racial Discrimination. Like most commitments towards fuller rights, the importance of the Convention was restricted by the requirement that its ratification was a voluntary action on the part of all the world's states. They were not in a hurry to sign: Britain did not adhere to the convention until 1969, and by 1976 it had been ratified by fewer than 90 of the U.N.'s 145 member-states. Naturally, the principal offenders against the Convention's code declined to assume this obligation.

While the Third World members of the U.N. succeeded in making South Africa into an international pariah, their efforts to liberate South West Africa – accorded recognition as Namibia – achieved no break-through.[12] In 1969 the U.N. passed resolution 269, calling on South Africa to vacate Namibia immediately. Two years later a reference by the U.N. to the International Court produced a series of legal opinions which reaffirmed the decisions taken in the General Assembly. In 1972, the U.N. Secretary-General Kurt Waldheim was invited by South Africa to visit Namibia. He reported to the U.N. in mid-1973, and thereafter the South African Prime Minister, Vorster, stated that he 'had no intention of delaying the act of self-determination'. He hinted that this self-determination would not come within ten years, but the revolution in Angola in 1975 had a dramatic influence upon the speed of the transfer in Namibia.

A new grouping emerged in 1976: the so-called 'Front-line Presidents', the leaders of Tanzania, Zambia, Botswana, Mozambique and Angola (see Map 2). Differing sharply in their internal policies they were united in their determination to end white domination in Southern Africa. Even the most moderate was committed to a struggle involving guerrilla warfare.

*

As we have noted, Israel has come to be pilloried at the U.N. almost as much as South Africa. But this casting of Israel in the role of racist occurred relatively belatedly, during the 1970s. The U.N. resolution which proposed the partition of Palestine into Jewish and Arab states in May 1948 was sponsored both by the United States and the Soviet Union: by the former in response to the demand of American Jewry, and by the latter because it was suspected that the Arab League was a client of British imperialism! Britain abstained over the issue, but the partition plan was opposed in the U.N. by the Arab members and by seven other countries, including India. Thus, from the beginning, Israel was in Third World eyes a creation of the superpowers and increasingly was viewed as an outpost of the West. However, it was not until the third Sinai war in 1967 that international opinion began to polarise against Israel. The consequences will be examined later.

During the 1950s and early 1960s the taint of racism adhered to the United States in a number of U.N. encounters. America's racist image must have become worse as the involvement in the Vietnam war intensified, but for the exclusion of 'Red' China from the U.N. As it was, the American – and British – reputation continued to be measured by the South African issue: as Harold Isaacs puts it: 'The dragging reluctance of Britain and the United States to join in these indictments – much less to take the actions voted – has served as a measure in the minds of many nonwhites (American as well as others) of the value of the commitments which these governments always make on the issues of equality and justice in general.'[13]

The issue which above all others seemed to emphasise the racial gulf in the 1950s and early 1960s was that of colonialism, both external and internal. Americans were convinced that they were guiltless on this issue, yet others were not so sure. Thus, the status of the American dependencies was not clear, even to friends of the United States. Concerning the degree of self-government enjoyed by Puerto Rico, 'serious doubts were expressed by some non-Communist members of the [U.N.] Assembly'.[14] When Adlai Stevenson as American Ambassador to the U.N. opposed the admission of Communist China on the grounds that people in China were not free, Ambassador Zorin of the Soviet Union observed: 'If the way citizens of a country are treated is a basis for membership of the U.N., then the United States should be voted out, because of her treatment of Negroes.'

When, in 1962, India pressed Portugal to hand over the territory of Goa, the Portuguese retorted that Goa was a province of Portugal. Adlai Stevenson endorsed this claim, and when Indian troops marched in to seize Goa he launched a blistering attack at the U.N. against Indian aggression. Most of Portugal's NATO partners joined in supporting this colonial anachronism, and Nehru commented bitterly: 'I do not like this division of opinion – to put it crudely, white and black. I do not like it at all. . . . We are developing a mentality of black against white, distrust of each other, dislike of each other, suspicion of each other.' Clearly, two forms of political moralising were in conflict. And it was the American form which was least in tune with the spirit of the age.

There were few delays in decolonisation, but some last controversies over colonialism, or neo-colonialism, were incurred with President Sukarno of Indonesia. Sukarno always dreamed of a Greater Indonesia, 'Independent Indonesia should extend to Malaya and Papua' he declared.[15] Stubbornly, the Dutch maintained their hold over West New Guinea, or West Irian as Indonesia called it. They resisted Indonesian retaliation, which involved the ejection of thousands of Dutch citizens and the expropriation of Dutch business, but they could not indefinitely resist the pressures exerted at the United Nations. Quite suddenly, the Netherlands announced that it would place West New Guinea under U.N. trusteeship. The U.N. took over, introducing administrators and soldiers from Third World countries. A perfunctory consultation of the local population was effected, and then in May 1963 the territory was handed over to Indonesia. U Thant, the U.N. Secretary-General, assured the local population that Indonesia would 'scrupulously observe' their right to self-determination. However, within four years villages in West Irian were under attack from the Indonesian Air Force.

Encouraged by his success in beating down the sturdy Dutch, Sukarno turned his attention to the territories in Borneo which Britain planned to hand over to a newly created Malaysia. Sukarno denounced the new federation as neo-colonial and coined the slogan 'crush Malaysia'. The issue was referred to the U.N., where the Soviet Union, along with many radical Third World allies, was prepared to endorse the Indonesian claim. But Malaysia had many friends in the U.N., both among Western and moderate Afro-Asian countries. Indonesia did not succeed in her claim. Frustrated also in the military campaign of 'Confrontation' (*Konfrontasi*), Sukarno took his country out of the U.N.: the only nation to walk out in its history.

China supported Indonesia's action. Chou En-lai, the Chinese Premier, declared: 'The United Nations has committed too many mistakes. It has utterly disappointed Afro-Asian countries. It must correct its mistakes. It must be reorganised.' Mr Chou observed that China, North Korea and North Vietnam were all kept outside the U.N.; and they made up more than a quarter of the world's population: 'In these circumstances another United Nations, a revolutionary one, may well be set up so that rival dramas may be staged in competition with that body which calls itself the United Nations but which is under the manipulation of United States imperialism and therefore can only make mischief.' Chou En-lai declared that the Indonesian people could not tolerate Malaysia, just as the Arab peoples could not tolerate Israel. He accused the United States of 'clamouring to enlarge the war in South East Asia . . . and trying to drag Britain along down in the mire. . . . Baring its fangs and showing its claws this paper tiger, United States imperialism, fancies itself to be formidable. But the Chinese people . . . only hold it to be quite miserable and ludicrous.'[16]

At this time, the portrayal of America to the Chinese people was frankly based upon an appeal to xenophobia and racism. Uncle Sam was depicted as a red-faced, cowardly buffoon, whose arrogant bluster would dissolve into cowardly snivelling when confronted by the bayonets of the People's Liberation Army. And yet, within a few years, Chou En-lai was announcing that the enemy was the revisionist Soviet Union. The dispute which caused the U.S.S.R. and China to form separate camps was as much racial as ideological. Russia responded to the old threat of the Yellow Peril, fearing that China would advance claims to all those lands which historically formed part of the Manchu Empire. China, on its side, saw the U.S.S.R. as a menacing new Eurocentric imperialist system. And so the stage was to be set for that amazing scene when Richard Nixon – once, most enthusiastic champion of the Dulles doctrine of the containment of communism – was received in Peking as the honoured guest of Chou En-lai, Chairman Mao and the People's Republic.

The transformation of the Sino-American relationship is the most dramatic example of an exception to the theme presented in this book that the international order is becoming polarised between the 'Haves', the white over-developed countries, and the 'Have-Nots', the black and brown underdeveloped countries and peoples. But, of course, history does not unfold on completely clear-cut lines. Fundamental divisions can become blurred by secondary considerations.

One such issue which came before the U.N. in 1968 was the future of Gibraltar. In this case the morality of condoning a vestige of colonialism had to be weighed against the morality of giving a boost to a decadent fascist regime. Spain demanded the return of the Rock; Britain rejected the demand on the ground that the inhabitants desired to remain British – and free. The vote in the General Assembly in December 1968 demonstrated that the emotional reaction against colonialism transcended other considerations: Britain lost the debate (for the vote had no mandatory power) by 67 votes to 18, with 34 abstentions.

The majority included all the Soviet bloc, several Latin-American states, and most of the Afro-Asians. Yet only four black and brown Commonwealth countries (Cyprus, Pakistan, Tanzania and Zambia) voted with the majority. Most of the non-white Commonwealth abstained (as did India, Kenya, Trinidad and Uganda) while eleven black and brown Commonwealth countries actually supported Britain, the other six supporters being white friends and neighbours (though the United States abstained to preserve its anti-colonial self-image). It is not often that black and brown solidarity is as split as over the Gibraltar resolution.

The legitimacy of guerrilla techniques is an issue that divides the U.N. upon lines that reflect racial as well as ideological groupings. When in 1972 the United States introduced a draft resolution on 'measures to prevent terrorism' the counter-argument was advanced that before terrorism could be eliminated the root causes must be recognised, 'namely colonialism, racialism, and occupation of land'. The resolution was referred to a committee where it was substantially amended to acknowledge the right of oppressed peoples to resist by all means, including force. The United States and other Western sponsors did not press the issue any further. Then, in 1974, the International Red Cross laid before the U.N. a draft protocol designed to cover situations of international armed conflict. This was another stage in the long endeavour by the Red Cross to make the conditions of war to some extent civilised. An amendment was put in by Afro-Asian countries to make the Red Cross provisions applicable to 'armed conflict in which peoples are fighting against colonial domination and alien occupation and against racist regimes in the exercise of their right of self-determination'. This amendment was, in effect, a licence to the guerrilla to go out and shoot: a right which they would emphatically deny to their own militant radicals. Nevertheless, this amendment was accepted by 70 votes to 21 against. Its significance was twofold. Black Africa served notice that the white occupation of Southern Africa could not continue, and if equality continued to be denied to the Africans the whites could expect to face an armed revolt. The Arabs served a similar notice on Israel. Secondly, the amendment asserted that international law was not merely designed to provide a framework for the established states, but was also to be employed to bestow legitimacy upon guerrillas and other groups who although operating at a sub-national level are operating on behalf of peoples denied freedom. The issue of race had added another dimension to international relations.

The emotional appeal of anti-colonialism, the causes of the under-dog, and the symbolic importance of race in conflicts which are essentially non-racial were illustrated by the U.N. vote on Cyprus in 1975, which followed the seizure by the Turkish forces of the north-eastern third of the island. By most kinds of group identification, the Greek-Orthodox Cypriots and the Turkish Muslim Cypriots all belong to the same eastern Mediterranean ethnic group. One might have supposed that any artificial attempt to fit Cyprus into a racial pattern would have identified the Greek Cypriots as the whites and the Turks as the blacks: certainly, their economic backwardness fitted them for the role of underdogs.

However, the underground struggle by EOKA against British rule, followed by the strong commitment of the regime of Archbishop Makarios to the Afro-Asian cause, created a sense of identity between Greek Cyprus and the radical regimes of Libya and Algeria, and more broadly with the Third World, overriding other considerations. It was not considered important that Makarios had close links with the fascist—militarist regime in Greece and himself employed semi-fascist methods against his opponents. When machinations instigated from Athens led to the downfall of Makarios and the attempt to impose a ruthlessly anti-Turkish regime upon the island, the Turkish Cypriots appealed to the government of Turkey, which by means of a two-phase operation managed to wrest territory from the Greek Cypriots up to the 'Attila Line'.

Despite official American opposition to the invasion, demonstrated by suspension of arms supplies to Turkey, most of the Third World accepted the charge by Makarios that the United States had connived at the Turkish action because of the importance of NATO bases in Turkey. When resolution 3395 was moved in 1975, calling upon Turkey to withdraw its forces from Cyprus, the sponsors were Algeria, Argentina, Guyana, India, Mali and Yugoslavia: a group broadly representative of the Third World and the non-aligned nations.

Turkey alone voted against the resolution and 117 states voted in support; previously, only the South African issue had aroused such a consensus throughout the U.N. The abstentions were few: Chile, the Gambia, Iran, Israel, Jordan, Morocco, Pakistan, Saudi Arabia and the United States (9). For most of these countries, Islamic solidarity provided the motive for abstaining, though others had their own reasons involving their own situations vis-à-vis the U.N.

The Cyprus issue demonstrates how a non-racial conflict can assume racial overtones, but the question of the Palestinians has provided the most powerful example of how race and racism can be injected into almost any conflict in which one side appears as the oppressor and the other as the oppressed.

For the Arab Palestinian refugees, the four wars between the Arab states and Israel brought no kind of relief. The 1967 war caused a second flight of the refugees (260,455 were displaced), and in 1974 there were 1,583,646 registered as recipients of relief by U.N.R.W.A. (the U.N. Relief and Works Agency for Palestine Refugees). Over half a million of the Palestinians were still living in refugee camps in 1974. For the Arab governments, the refugees were little more than pawns in the struggle against Israel.* As a result of the 1973 war, Egypt obtained the reopening of the Suez Canal, but not a single refugee benefited. The Palestinians realised that they must rely upon their own resources.

All the *fedayin* recognise the overall authority of the Palestine Liberation Organisation founded in 1964 as the political wing of their movement. The largest guerrilla force is that of *Al Fateh* ('Victorious')

* The sums of aid given for refugee relief by the major donors, 1950 – 74, are stated to be U.S.A., $577 million; Britain, $133 million; Canada, $32 million; Germany, $27 million. The U.S.S.R. made no contribution. By contrast, Egypt contributed $5·5 million; Saudi Arabia, $5·4 million; Jordan, $3·4 million (mostly received from outside); Syria, $2·2 million; Lebanon, $1·3 million; Iraq, $975,000. Source: Martin Gilbert, *The Jews of Arab Lands: Their History in Maps* (London, 1975)

which has received some aid from Algeria but is undeniably a Palestinian strike-force. Its claims have not always been accepted. King Hussain of Jordan sees *Al Fateh* as a threat to his throne and to his kingdom, and in 1970 in what was called 'Black September' his army fell upon the *fedayin*, expelling them and destroying their power. *Al Fateh* was re-formed and attracts massive support. Its activities in Lebanon also led to containment by the Lebanese army and a belated attempt by the Christian *Falange* to carry out a coup similar to that of the Black September. Instead, the Palestinians in Lebanon (numbering at least 200,000) combined with left-wing forces to attack and liquidate the coalition government of Christians and Muslims which has maintained a fragile neutrality in Lebanon between the pressure of the Arab states and Israel. Counter-moves by Syria were seen by the Palestinians as another 'Black September', and the combined intervention of the Arab League states was needed to enforce a precarious truce late in 1976.

After the achievements of the *fedayin* during the early 1970s, it was impossible for any of the parties in the conflict – the Arabs, the Israelis, the Russians and the West – to think they could leave the Palestinians to rot in their camps. Although the areas which were their strongholds until 1967, around Hebron and Nablus (the so-called West Bank) had passed into Israeli military occupation, they have defied the Israelis and rallied under the P.L.O. banner. They have succeeded in making the Arab governments listen to the P.L.O., and they have seen the P.L.O. accepted at the United Nations as the principal party in the conflict. Yasser Arafat told the assembled delegates that he came bearing a gun and an olive branch; he offered Israel the choice of war or a negotiated peace. As a first step towards peace, Israel should transfer the Gaza strip and the West Bank to P.L.O. control.[17] Should there be no response, evidence of the capacity to make trouble was provided by the move to isolate the Israelis in the U.N., as South Africa had been isolated, by branding them as pariahs.

The charge was the same – racism – and in November 1975 there was a symbolic victory when, on the initiative of the more militant Arabs, the U.N. voted 'Yes' to a resolution describing Zionism 'as a form of racism and racial discrimination'. The vote showed 72 states for the resolution, 35 against, and 32 abstentions. Considering the gravity of the charge, the majority was large, and included China and other Asian countries, more than half the Africans, the Soviet bloc, and also Brazil, Cyprus, Malta, Mexico, Portugal and Turkey. The main opponents were the United States, the European community and Britain. (Britain announced that it might review its adherence to the Convention on Racial Discrimination in view of the interpretation adopted by the Arabs.) Their counter-attacks carried the allegation that the resolution was anti-Semitic; but this was hotly denied, and a distinction was drawn by Third World speakers between Zionism and Judaism.*

The American Ambassador at the U.N., Daniel P. Moynihan, was moved to make a massive counter-demonstration against the Third World. He accused General Amin of Uganda (one of Israel's noisiest critics) of being a racist and he dismissed the pretensions of the new states to be democracies, comparing Israel's record to its advantage. Moynihan acquired a good deal of popularity with the American public especially among the ethnics, who saw the attack upon Israel as evidence yet again of how black and brown people obtained easy advantages by denouncing white racism, whatever the facts. Moynihan's Irish ardour was not endorsed by President Ford, nor by Henry Kissinger with his German-Jewish realism.† Moynihan resigned, and Kissinger soon found himself contronted in Angola with the consequences of a successful combination of Soviet military aid, Cuban fighting strength, and African national feeling. His first response was somewhat bland and inadequate. He tried to restore American standing in Black Africa by means of one of his whirlwind capital-hopping trips. Pausing in Lusaka, he announced that the United States would triple its development programme in Southern and Central Africa over the next three years: it was the old, outworn formula.

* Without condoning any aspect of the attack upon Zionism it has to be accepted that Israeli society does contain separate elements, which may be described as racial divisions as the term is understood in Britain. The European Jews have a superior status, if measured by higher education, or employment in the professions, and other higher-income jobs. The so-called 'Oriental Jews' (originating from the countries of North Africa, the Levant, and the Near East) are not only at an economic disadvantage but also have to overcome social prejudices. Most juvenile crime is ascribed to the Moroccan Jews. The Arabs – Muslims, Christians and Druses – are second-class citizens in Israel in most ways. Their strength lies partly in the growing proportion of the population of Israel which they represent, due to higher birthrates. For those Israelis to whom the European quality of national life is important, the movement of Jews from the Soviet Union is therefore vital, for they represent the last great reservoir of Western Jewry.

† American foreign policy is always said to be susceptible to pressure from 'the Three Is' – Israel, Ireland and Italy – whose people are in strategic strength among the American electorate. The Israeli factor in American foreign policy is an acknowledged absolute. Ireland is important in Boston, and Teddy Kennedy can be relied upon to denounce British oppression, but Ireland scarcely affects the over-all making of foreign policy. Italy appears to play no part in the calculations of the State Department.

However, Kissinger's strength was his ability to grasp when a historical moment of change was imminent. In September 1976 he set out again for Africa on what was to prove one of his most historic missions.

It will be remembered that when the Bandung conference condemned the racialism inherent in Western colonialism, it also undertook to eradicate racial practices in the Third World. Yet these practices have persisted, and increased, without any great outcry against them. In the nineteenth century, both China and India observed that the Western world applied severe racialist policies against the emigrants who left their shores, and the experience contributed substantially to the rise of a demand for equality between peoples from the two largest countries of Asia. In the twenty years after the Second World War, people who had originally emigrated from China and India were subjected to discrimination and persecution in several of the new Afro-Asian states. The Asian giants chose to ignore all these cases of wrong within the Third World.

The overseas Chinese of South-east Asia have endured unequal treatment and at times have endured race riots in most of the countries of the region. Their predominance in trade and industry has brought upon them retaliatory policies of economic nationalism designed to transfer some of their prosperity to the sons of the soil. The threat which they are supposed to pose as a political fifth column (whether as agents of Taiwan or Peking) has brought bloody retaliation upon them. In Indonesia in 1963, and in Malaysia in 1969, they were targets for slaughter by enraged Malay rioters. The reaction of the great People's Republic to these attacks upon the overseas Chinese has been scarcely perceptible. For China, good relations with the South-east Asian governments has been more important than any attempt to champion the overseas communities.

India has reacted in precisely the same fashion when overseas Indians have been persecuted. When about half-a-million Indians were expelled from Burma the Indian government made no protest, and when General Amin adopted identical tactics against the Asians in Uganda the Indian government at first regarded the expulsions as not being its affair. The denial of political and civil rights to a million people of Indian origin in Sri Lanka has been the subject of sporadic negotiation between India and Sri Lanka, but when these have yielded no benefit to the Ceylon Indians there has been no move to consider any kind of sanctions.[18] Similarly, the systematic deprivation of Indians in Kenya of economic and civil rights has been ignored by the Government of India.

The fact that a country has acted harshly against Chinese or Indian residents seems to form no obstacle if diplomatic or trade negotiations are to follow. Having suppressed Chinese political parties and trade unions in Malaysia in 1969, the ruling Malay hardliners went on to hold successful trade negotiations at Peking two years later. On the other hand, it has been argued that it is actually an impediment to closer relations between China and Singapore that the island-city is virtually a Chinese outpost. Singapore holds back from closer ties with Peking so as not to appear 'a Chinese island in a Malay sea'.[19]

Hence, race and racism among non-whites has not been an issue in the relations between Third World states or in their perception of what ought to be brought before the United Nations. Concern for the right of repressed peoples to fight for their liberty has not included the black tribes of South Sudan who struggled for ten years against the army sent to subdue them by the Nilotic northerners, nor has it included the Kurds, fighting for their own state against the forces of Iraq.

Meanwhile, the conflict between white and black, sometimes grimly explicit, though often merely implicit, intensified during the summer of 1976. The centrality of Africa to this conflict became even more evident. Once again, South Africa provided the flashpoint. Protests by black students at having to acquire their education in the Afrikaans language were ignored by the Nationalist government. The protests escalated into an outbreak of violent protest in Soweto township, one of the satellite black towns serving Johannesburg. In the subsequent confrontations with police and army, more Africans were killed than in the shootings at Sharpeville.

The killings were angrily denounced by the leaders of the African states, meeting in Mauritius at the O.A.U. Summit in June 1976. The Western press was severely critical, but Western leaders made no move. New Zealand, with an insensitivity due more to its isolation from the contemporary scene than to a deliberate assertion of white solidarity, despatched a rugby football team to tour South Africa almost immediately after the Soweto killings. When the Olympic sportsmen gathered at Montreal in July, the Africans demanded that the New Zealand team should withdraw. New Zealand refused; and more than twenty African teams – supported by Guyana – quit the Olympic Games.[20] The future of world sport looked distinctly uncertain against the strains of racial conflict.

When the Movement of Non-Aligned Nations held its summit meetings in Sri Lanka in August 1976, the repression in South Africa was severely condemned, and a strong call was made for a U.N. arms embargo. The Non-Aligned communiqué condemned Britain, West Germany and France for their continuing economic support of White South Africa, but the strongest condemnation was reserved for Israel which had supplied arms to the Vorster government. The U.N. resolution denouncing Zionism as a form of racism was reaffirmed by the Movement (although a few states expressed reservations). An ideological link between South Africa and Israel as the two outlaws of white racism was thus more closely emphasised by the representatives of the black and brown world.

Another milestone in the symbolic isolation of South Africa was reached when, in November 1976, ten harshly critical resolutions were adopted in the U.N. General Assembly. One declared that 'the oppressed people of South Africa' have no alternative but to resort to armed struggle to achieve their rights: once again, the legitimacy of guerrilla action against racist regimes was reaffirmed. Another strongly condemned 'the continuing and increasing collaboration of Israel with the South African racist regime': once again, Israel was labelled as racist by association. Yet another resolution, adopted by 128 votes to none (with 12 abstentions), called for an international convention against apartheid in sports and for the refusal of all assistance to sporting contacts with South Africa. New Zealand acquiesced in the motion, abandoning the long-held policy of 'keeping politics out of sport'.[21] All the strands in the Third World's struggle against racism were becoming interwoven.

*

In the aftermath of the Angola civil war, the white mercenaries hired by the defeated side were put on trial with massive publicity designed to attract world attention. All the mercenaries were found guilty and four were condemned to death. There was an outcry in Britain and America, in which leading politicians joined, demanding that the death sentences be commuted. When it is recalled that the mercenary leader, the self-styled Colonel Callan, had presided over many executions, including those of his own soldiers, one has to conclude that the demand was made not because those under sentence were innocent but because they were white. The condemned men were shot: and in the case of an American mercenary who had been in Angola only a few days without firing a weapon, one also has to conclude that he was shot not because of his crimes but because he was a white American. Racial enmity has two faces.

When Palestinian guerrillas in July 1976 hijacked an Air France plane carrying Israeli passengers, and flew to Entebbe in Uganda, a drama unfolded in which suspicion mounted that President Idi Amin was assisting the Palestinians. Not only did they demand the release of terrorists under sentence in Israel and West Germany in exchange for the hostages, but also they demanded the liberation of Ugandans imprisoned in Kenya for trying to assassinate President Kenyatta.

The long-drawn-out drama was terminated by an Israeli air-commando raid which rescued the hostages: and the international reaction was predictably mixed. African leaders condemned the violation of Uganda's sovereignty by Israel, while President Ford loudly applauded the dash and daring of the Israeli paratroopers. Britain's approval of the action was much more cautiously expressed; nevertheless, Amin's fury was mainly directed at Britain and at Kenya, where the Israeli plane refuelled after the Entebbe attack. The action of Kenya was explained by Amin to the people of Uganda by declaring 'They are not Africans'. As in Cyprus, where Turkish Cypriots could be symbolically identified as white, so in this African imbroglio it was desirable to suggest that Kenya was tinged with ideological whiteness.

Britain was accused of collusion with Israel, and British diplomats were expelled. In reply, Britain severed relations with Uganda. Amin announced that if any of the 200 Britons remaining in Uganda approached him they must do so on their knees, as British administrators were alleged to have made Baganda tribal leaders do in the early days. Field-Marshal (formerly Corporal) Amin is well aware that racialism has two faces.

*

Time after time, the debate about racism and white dominance returns to Southern Africa, the great white redoubt. Even B. J. Vorster, the hardline premier of South Africa, has to take notice of world pressures. His response, however, seems to resemble that of the legendary man on the sledge in frozen Russia, pursued by a pack of wolves, who tries to ensure his own safety by throwing out his children for the wolves to devour, thus slowing them down. Suddenly, in 1976, both Rhodesia and Namibia became expendable, in that order.

In consequence, the world was surprised by what seemed to be a complete 'about-turn' by Ian Smith and his government. The formidable combination of stick and carrot presented by Kissinger and Vorster proved effective where the casuistry of Harold Wilson and other British negotiators had failed. On 24 September 1976, Smith announced that he accepted Kissinger's terms, which appeared to concede a handover to an African government within two years. Kissinger offered compensations. Sanctions would be lifted, while an American – British – South African trust fund would be endowed to guarantee the economic interests of whites who stayed on in Rhodesia when it became Zimbabwe. Doubtless Kissinger could 'deliver' these promises, but in assuring Smith that the guerrilla war would be ended he went outside his own resources.

In the West there was applause for Kissinger's sensational coup; but from the Africans only a guarded welcome. The 'front-line presidents', and also the spokesmen of the guerrillas, insisted that an essential preliminary to ending the underground struggle was to reach a settlement in which African demands were accepted; and these did not include any remnant of white dominance in government and law-enforcement. Some Africans went further, demanding a radical restructuring of the Rhodesian economy.

The situation demonstrated that a gulf of misunderstanding still loomed between white and black. The former now talked about a multi-racial society and 'a Rhodesia for all Rhodesians'. They could not grasp that whether the future Zimbabwe evolved on the neo-capitalist lines of Kenya, the co-operative, socialist lines of Tanzania, or as a mixed economy like Zambia, the direction would ultimately be determined by African leaders. Smith's announcement of 24 September had appeared to recognise the end of white privilege. Yet there were still enormous, if unspoken, white reservations.

The process of working towards a solution was fraught with obstacles: yet for the whites there really could be no turning back. The white determination to uphold their cherished way of life had no long-term meaning after Ian Smith's dignified but undisguisable capitulation.

There had come a moment in Vietnam when Americans were not prepared any more to die – or even to endure hardship – for a goal that was clearly no longer attainable. White Rhodesians might prove more tenacious; but they would also discover that there was a point beyond which the fight against the guerrillas, involving the deaths of settlers and their sons, no longer had any meaning. By the end of 1976, the African guerrillas had not won in Rhodesia in any military sense: indeed, they could not occupy a single village inside the country. Yet, by creating stalemate, and by arousing the fear of the United States that the conflict would be internationalised and communised, they had gained the upper hand. What remained to be settled was whether Ian Smith would be able to accommodate essentially moderate leaders such as Abel Muzorewa and achieve a constitutional breakthrough, or whether the guerrilla leadership behind the Mozambique border would take over, continuing the struggle in order to fulfil the legend of the black man's defiant fight to vanquish white tyranny.

Suddenly, in the later 1970s, the importance of race in international conflict has become startlingly clear. But is there any pattern to it all? This study has offered a chronological narrative of events and trends in the twentieth century. In the concluding chapter we try to arrive at a conceptual analysis of the whole question.

7 The Racial Spiral

DURING the twentieth century the world order, the international system, has been transformed from a system in which all the proceedings were defined by those in control (the Strong) into one in which the rhetoric – and to some extent the reality – is defined by the non-white majority (the Many). This transformation occurred after the century was more than half-way through. During the first three decades the world order was still, effectively, the European or white order.

The first great upset to this order was brought about by the Japanese overthrow of Western dominance in East Asia. But Japanese 'co-prosperity' lasted less than four years. Then the world was split by the ideological confrontation between the United States and the Soviet Union (which some inspired abbreviators refer to as the US and the SU). Partly because of American pressure, more because of internal weaknesses, and ultimately because of the demands of the colonised, the Western empires went into liquidation. The Soviet Union gave powerful support to the decolonisation ethos and so, from 1960 onward, the non-white world had an increasing voice in the international arena.

For this Third World the memory of white dominance provided the principal political or ideological motivation. The concept of racism was enunciated, and was exported, into the former imperial metropolitan bastions, where it was seized upon by the black and brown population living almost like colonial workers in the urban centres. Guilt concerning white racism became a feature of the outlook of the white Establishment's race relations industry. It has not gained acceptance among the mass of the white population.

During the first three decades of the twentieth century there was still a concentration of political power and economic wealth and ideological initiative in Western Europe and North America. Because these three forms of dominance were fused together within the white – predominantly Anglo – segment of the world, it was this segment which commanded the world's response. It remained natural for a neo-Darwinian belief in a hierarchy of peoples to persist, with white ascendancy as an accepted feature of the international scene.

Already it was clear that there were non-whites who rejected this order of things. The 'problem of race' emerged out of their challenge. The dominant order declared that the 'race problem' was created by agitators among the black and brown people of the world, to make trouble, to disturb the processes of good government and the social order ordained by the whites.

Even in the 1970s there remains a conviction among many in America and Europe that there is a 'Negro problem' or an 'Asian problem'. Before the Second World War hardly anyone in the West questioned this conclusion, because it was the whites who were insisting that there was a problem, created by the non-whites trying to invade *their* domain. The relative status of white, brown and black was defined exclusively by the dominant group, in terms of their natural right to this dominance. The subservience of the rest was still rationalised in terms of their unfitness, their backwardness, their lack of moral fibre.

For example, in British India in 1906 and 1907, as the fiftieth anniversary of the Sepoy Revolt drew near, there was much discussion in ruling British circles about the growing assertiveness of the educated Indians. In the correspondence columns of the English-owned newspapers there were frequent references to this disturbing new feature. 'What is the theme of conversation, of thought, of correspondence among Europeans?' asked one contributor: 'The race problem. . . . Who that remembers the courteous, respectful native gentleman of forty years ago can feel anything but abhorrence for his decadent son or grandson.' Another correspondent wrote to agree: 'The educated or half-educated natives are the stirrers-up of strife and opposition. In a sensible race, it would and should be otherwise. . . . The Japanese . . . have raised themselves from serfdom and obscurity by their own Western spirit.'[1]

The 'race problem', then, was the problem of the non-white who would not accept the leadership of the white. Change could only be achieved by the almost impossible feat of actually securing political and economic equality with the whites. Japan had attained this equality: yet the attempt to get this formally recognised in the Treaty of Versailles was brushed aside by Japan's white allies. Japan only gained the desired status by military conquest in the Second World War.

When the terms 'racialist' and 'racialism' entered the English language between the two world wars, they were applied to those who sought to overturn white dominance, whether in the domestic politics of the American South or in the context of Western colonialism. When

Governor Mitchell of Kenya observed in 1945 that there was 'much intemperate racialism' in the colonial legislature, he meant that the Indian and African members were challenging the hitherto un-challenged ascendancy of the whites.[2]

After the Second World War, the declared commitment to freedom of Western liberalism was challenged by the commitment to revolution of Soviet communism. As the two blocs became increasingly monolithic and immobile, the claims of the Asians and then the Africans to independence and equality were important issues in the cold war. The first big test of the bona fides of each side at the United Nations in 1946 found the Communist bloc unequivocally supporting India in oppo-sition to White South Africa. The United States, the British Commonwealth, and most of the other Western members of the U.N. supported South Africa; ostensibly on legal grounds, but fundamentally because of their economic investment in South Africa and their tacit, implicit acceptance of the right of white people to rule.

Gradually, over the next two decades, the West had to become reconciled to the novel idea of independence for Asia and Africa. The process of adjustment was helped by certain illusions. The British supposed that the new Commonwealth would be much like the old Empire; the Americans assumed that they had a special role to play in economic aid, whereby the backwardness of colonialism would rapidly be replaced in the new countries by something like the American private-enterprise system (a kind of 'prosperity without tears').

Disillusionment was not slow in coming. Britain became involved in the insoluble complexities of Rhodesia, where white and black objectives appeared irreconcilable. The United States saw the death of most of the American dream in the long agony of Vietnam. Before this disillusionment had taken over, though, decolonisation was an accom-plished fact. Out of the old empires some ninety new states – almost all brown and black – took their place in the international arena, seeing their main forum of action as the United Nations.

Political élites in the West soon learned to accommodate their international style to the unfamiliar world of the Many. They quickly realised that open identification with White South Africa could only lead to 'guilt by association'. They quickly learnt the new rhetoric of inter-national equality and assimilated the new word, racism, into their vocabulary. Somewhat grudgingly, they even accepted that this was synonymous with white racism.[3]

It was inconvenient that the decade of decolonisation, 1960–70, coincided with a mass movement of Third World peoples into the urban centres of the West. While the political élites were learning the new language of multi-racialism the metropolitan masses were confronting their new brown and black neighbours and were rapidly learning (or remembering) the language of racial enmity. The disjunction between Establishment pronouncements and popular attitudes within Western societies was to be one cause of the populist white blacklash; directed against black people, and also against white governments.

There is a greater disjunction between the internal situation in Western countries where black and brown people are objects of discrimination, and the international stage where racism is universally condemned, and all the states are accorded the outward signs of equal status (whether at the U.N. or in the Commonwealth or other trans-national associations). An awareness of the contradictions between white attitudes and actions at these different levels disturbs and confounds international relations.

In addition – and perhaps of greater weight – there is the continuing economic dominance of the West in Africa and Asia. Despite the glib statements of British public men expressing opposition to apartheid, British investment in the South African economy (which means perpetuating the structure of white privilege and black exploitation) is undiminished. Similarly, British investment in former colonial territories like Kenya and Malaysia ensures that economic control remains when political control has lapsed.[4]

It follows that black and brown nations are conscious of still being the dependants and clients of their former white colonial masters. In the response of black and brown people as individuals and groups within the metropolitan white society, where they are depressed (and often oppressed) minorities, they may feel driven to negative forms of protest: that is, to violence and what the whites call crime. It seems probable that in their frustration some black and brown members of the world-order may react in similar ways.

Black and brown consciousness of the enormity of the domination, discrimination and deprivation still practised to preserve racial ascendancy fosters a tolerance, and indeed approval, of violent techniques in the name of the elimination of racism. Increasingly, advocates argue that violence is an essential tool in obtaining racial justice in white society – and beyond, in the international struggle. The claims of racial justice transcend the claims of international law. The white and black nations with their increasingly opposed views of rights and wrongs cannot agree upon international objectives (as debates in the U.N. Security Council clearly demonstrate). Though driven onto the defensive, the Western, white states will not give way to the new, non-white interpretation of the message of the times. There is a growing danger of international deadlock, as in the bleakest days of the cold war. Though the Many often will not be able to realise their demands, they are in a position to block or abort Western objectives.

Meanwhile, the new states will exploit such international institutions as they can, with ever-increasing emphasis upon refashioning the United Nations. Despite the persistence of inter-national conflicts among the Third World states it is probable that the urge to combine against the identified racial enemy – whether it is South Africa and the black Africans, or Israel and the Arabs – will always be stronger than pressures to differ, based upon national ideology or national interest (as between Uganda and Kenya, or Egypt and Syria).

Any significant modification of the present line-up of international forces can only emerge from fundamental changes in the economic and social policies of the nations of North America and Western Europe. Of this, there is no sign; and so the cleavages between the West and the Third World can only intensify. Hence, the Soviet Union will continue to be perceived by many as a friend and ally, even when (as in Angola) the U.S.S.R. is carrying out an imperialistic mission. However, the immunity of the U.S.S.R. from the charge of racism may not last for ever, and the rise of China as leader of the Third World – which gains momentum almost imperceptibly, yet continuously – will gradually work to change the image of the U.S.S.R. in black and brown countries. It is fruitless to speculate upon this still unrealised change.

What is certain is that the race spiral becomes ever steeper. Race operates at every level and in almost every context. Down to the 1950s it was possible to regard relations between races as fixed, permanent: or, alternatively, in many countries or areas, to dismiss race as something that affected others but not one's own condition. From about 1960, race entered into the experience of everybody (even the competitors in the Miss World Beauty Competition of 1976, when girls were withdrawn in protest against South Africa). The very different reactions of different people, different communities, all became part of the total experience. This is still a new idea to many.

There will be those who imagine that if the Rhodesian time-bomb can be defused then the racial factor in international politics will recede. The first over-dramatic reaction to the Kissinger success was that he had 'averted a race war in Southern Africa'. All that Kissinger actually did in September 1976 was to succeed in bringing Ian Smith face to face with realities evident since the early 1960s and the 'winds of change'. The cleavage between white and black in Southern Africa continues.

Race does not recognise frontiers, and Vorster's attempt to seem liberal abroad while remaining reactionary at home does not stand a chance. Where race is the issue, nobody can stop the clock. The bell tolls for South Africa also: and not only for South Africa, for by 'operation-alising' the powerful though diffused forces of resistance to racism, African leaders have shown how the powerless may disarm the powerful. Their example may be followed later in the century in the Caribbean, in Latin America, and above all, in the Middle East. Race may become the Achilles' heel of the West, and of North America especially. The dramatic events of 1976 may not have an immediate sequel. But they are demonstrations of the long-term trend.

In seventeenth-century Europe, religion formed the total experience. Transcending everything – dynastic struggles, political debates, artistic and literary ferment, the rise of capitalism, the challenge of science and rationalism – was the confrontation between Catholicism and Protestantism. Today, transcending everything (including even the nuclear threat) there is the confrontation between the races. This will spiral on, inexorably, as the twentieth century moves to its end.

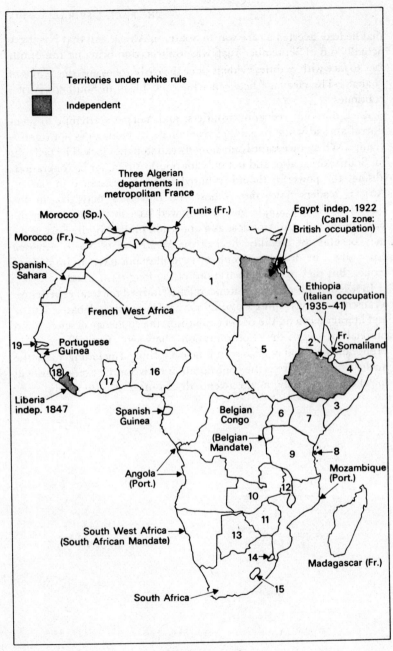

Territories under white rule

Independent

Morocco (Sp.)

Morocco (Fr.)

Three Algerian
departments in
metropolitan France

Tunis (Fr.)

Egypt indep. 1922
(Canal zone:
British occupation)

Spanish
Sahara

French West Africa

1

5

Ethiopia
(Italian occupation
1935–41)

2

Fr.
Somaliland

4

19

Portuguese
Guinea

16

18

17

Liberia
indep. 1847

Spanish
Guinea

3

6

7

Belgian
Congo

(Belgian
Mandate)

8

9

Mozambique
(Port.)

Angola
(Port.)

10

12

11

South West Africa
(South African Mandate)

13

14

Madagascar (Fr.)

South Africa

15

AFRICA IN 1946

British Colonies, Protectorates, and Occupied Territories in 1946

1. Libya (formerly Italian)
2. Eritrea (formerly Italian)
3. Somaliland (formerly Italian)
4. British Somaliland
5. Anglo-Egyptian Sudan
6. Uganda
7. Kenya
8. Zanzibar
9. Tanganyika
10. Northern Rhodesia
11. Southern Rhodesia
12. Nyasaland
13. Bechuanaland
14. Swaziland
15. Basutoland
16. Nigeria
17. Gold Coast
18. Sierra Leone
19. The Gambia

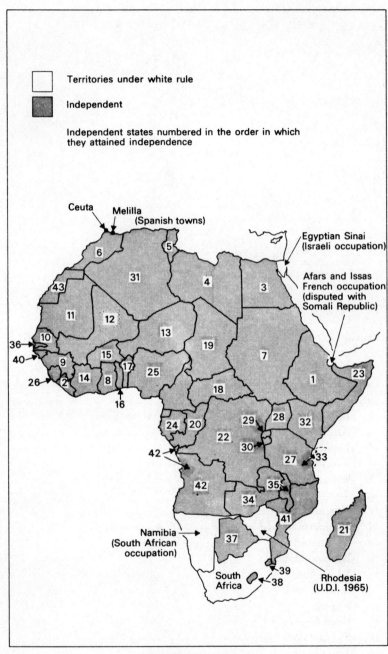

Territories under white rule

Independent

Independent states numbered in the order in which
they attained independence

Ceuta   Melilla
(Spanish towns)

Egyptian Sinai
(Israeli occupation)

Afars and Issas
French occupation
(disputed with
Somali Republic)

Namibia
(South African
occupation)

South
Africa

Rhodesia
(U.D.I. 1965)

AFRICA IN 1976

Africa in 1976 (Dates of Independence)

1. Ethiopia, 2nd century A.D. (incorporating Eritrea, 1948)
2. Liberia, 1847
3. Egypt (United Arab Republic), 1922
4. Libya, 1951
5. Tunisia, 1956
6. Morocco, 1956
7. Sudan, 1956
8. Ghana, 1957
9. Guinea, 1958
10. Senegal, 1960
11. Mauretania, 1960
12. Mali, 1960
13. Niger, 1960
14. Ivory Coast, 1960
15. Upper Volta, 1960
16. Togo, 1960
17. Dahomey, 1960
18. Central African Republic, 1960
19. Chad, 1960
20. Congo (Brazzaville), 1960
21. Malagasy Republic, 1960
22. Zaire, 1960
23. Somali Republic (former Italian and British Somaliland), 1960
24. Gabon, 1960
25. Nigeria, 1960
26. Sierra Leone, 1961
27. Tanganyika, 1961
28. Uganda, 1962
29. Rwanda, 1962
30. Burundi, 1962
31. Algeria, 1962
32. Kenya, 1963
33. Zanzibar, 1963 (incorporated with Tanganyika as Tanzania, 1964)
34. Zambia, 1964
35. Malawi, 1964
36. The Gambia, 1965
37. Botswana, 1966
38. Lesotho, 1966
39. Swaziland, 1968
40. Guinea-Bissau, 1975
41. Mozambique, 1975
42. Angola, 1975
43. Sahara, 1976 (union with Morocco)

Further Reading

THIS booklist is not intended as a conventional bibliography: as indicated in the Preface, there are no other complete book-length studies on the international aspects of race. Chapter 2 is covered by the section immediately below, but the other sections do not relate to chapters of the book. They deal with subjects which have significant connections with the international theme. Some titles included are by people involved in racial conflicts: these are marked with an asterisk (*). Reports of the Minority Rights Group are marked M.R.G. Several novels are included, for race at its deepest level is evoked most profoundly in imaginative literature.

RACE AND EMPIRE

CHRISTINE BOLT, *Victorian Attitudes to Race* (London, 1971).

C. R. BOXER, *Race Relations in the Portuguese Colonial Empire*, (Oxford, 1963).

E. M. FORSTER, *A Passage to India* (London, 1924) (novel).

R. A. HUTTENBACK, *Racism and Empire: White Settlers and Colored Immigrants in the British Self-Governing Colonies, 1830–1910* (Ithaca, N.Y., 1976).

WINTHROP JORDAN, *White over Black* (Chapel Hill, N. Carolina, 1968).

V. G. KIERNAN, *The Lords of Human Kind* (London, 1969).

PHILIP MASON, *Patterns of Dominance* (London, 1970).

ROLAND OLIVER, *The Missionary Factor in East Africa* (London, 1952).

GEORGE ORWELL, *Burmese Days* (London, 1935) (novel).

K. M. PANIKKAR, *Asia and Western Dominance* (London, 1953).

CHARLES A. PRICE, *The Great White Walls are Built: Restrictive Immigration to North America and Australasia, 1836–1888* (Canberra, 1974).

HUGH TINKER, *A New System of Slavery: the Export of Indian Labour Overseas, 1830–1920* (London, 1974).

——, *Separate and Unequal: India and the Indians in the British Commonwealth, 1920–1950* (London, 1976).

GUY WINT, *The British in Asia* (London, 1947).

*

RACE AND INDIVIDUAL COUNTRIES AND AREAS

Australia

AMIRAH INGLIS, *Not a White Woman Safe: Sexual Anxiety and Politics in Port Moresby* (Canberra, 1974). (Also published by Sussex U.P. as *The White Women's Protection Ordinance*, 1975).

H. I. LONDON, *Non-Western Immigration and the 'White Australia' Policy* (New York, 1970).

Britain

SHEILA ALLEN, *New Minorities, Old Conflicts* (New York, 1971).

PAUL FOOT, *Immigration and Race in British Politics* (London, 1965).

RUTH GLASS, *Newcomers* (London, 1960).

BOB HEPPLE, *Race, Jobs and the Law in Britain* (London, 1968).

J. R. LAMBERT, *Crime, Police and Race Relations: A Study in Birmingham* (London, 1970).

KENNETH LITTLE, *Negroes in Britain* (London, 1948).

KAMALA MARKANDAYA, *The Nowhere Man* (London, 1972) (novel).

* CHRIS MULLARD, *Black Britain* (London, 1973).

JOHN REX AND ROBERT MOORE, *Race, Community and Conflict: A Study of Sparkbrook* (London, 1967).

* SAMUEL SELVON, *The Lonely Londoners* (London, 1956) (novel).

* URSULA SHARMA, *Rampal and his Family* (London, 1971).

Canada

TED FERGUSON, *A White Man's Country: An Exercise in Canadian Prejudice* (Toronto, 1975).

D. R. HUGHES AND EVELYN KALLEN, *The Anatomy of Racism: Canadian Dimensions* (Montreal, 1974).

JAMES WILSON, *Canada's Indians* (London, 1974) (M.R.G.).

Caribbean

WENDELL BELL (ed.), *The Democratic Revolution in the West Indies* (Cambridge, Mass., 1967).

EDOUARD GLISSANT, *Le Quatrième Siècle* (Paris, 1962) (novel).

B. A. INCE, *Decolonization and Conflict in the United Nations: Guyana's Struggle for Independence* (Cambridge, Mass., 1974).

* CHEDDI JAGAN, *The West on Trial* (London, 1966).

* GEORGE LAMMING, *In the Castle of My Skin* (London, 1953) (novel).

DAVID LOWENTHAL, *West Indian Societies* (London, 1972).

A. R. PREISWERK, *Regionalism and the Commonwealth Caribbean* (Trinidad, 1968).

SELWYN RYAN, *Race and Nation in Trinidad and Tobago: A Study of Decolonisation in a Multi-racial Society* (Toronto, 1972).

M. G. SMITH, *The Plural Society in the British West Indies* (Berkeley, Calif., 1965).

TAD SZULO (ed.,), *The United States and the Caribbean* (Englewood Cliffs, N.J., 1971).

East Africa

PREM BHATIA, *Indian Ordeal in Africa* (Delhi, 1973).

DHARAM P. GHAI (ed.), *Portrait of a Minority: Asians in East Africa* (Nairobi, 1965).

GERALD HANLEY, *Drinkers of Darkness* (London, 1973) (novel).

* JOMO KENYATTA, *Suffering without Bitterness* (Nairobi, 1968).

LEO KUPER AND M. G. SMITH (eds), *Pluralism in Africa* (Berkeley, Calif., 1969).

COLIN LEYS, *Underdevelopment in East Africa: The Political Economy of Neo-colonialism, 1964–1971* (London, 1975).

NORMAN LEYS, *The Colour Bar in East Africa* (London, 1941).

* TOM MBOYA, *Freedom and After* (London, 1963).

* O. ODINGA, *Not Yet Uhuru* (London, 1967).

MICHAEL TWADDLE (ed.), *Expulsion of a Minority: Essays on Ugandan Asians* (London, 1975).

India and Ceylon

MULK RAJ ANAND, *Untouchable* (London, 1935) (novel).

N. B. BONARJEE, *Under Two Masters* (Calcutta, 1970).

*NIRAD C. CHAUDHURI, *The Autobiography of an Unknown Indian* (London, 1951).

B. H. FARMER, *Ceylon, a Divided Nation* (London, 1963).

HAROLD ISAACS, *India's Ex-Untouchables* (New York, 1964).

——, *Scratches on Our Minds: American Images of China and India* (New York, 1958).

RUTH PRAWER JHABVALA, *Heat and Dust* (London, 1975) (novel).

D. E. SMITH, *India as a Secular State* (Princeton, N.J., 1963).

A. JEYARATNAM WILSON, *Politics in Sri Lanka, 1947–1963* (New York, 1974).

South-east Asia

GARTH ALEXANDER, *Silent Invasion: Overseas Chinese in South East Asia* (London, 1973).

S. ARASARATNAM, *Indians in Malaysia and Singapore* (London, 1970).

N. R. CHAKRAVARTI, *The Indian Minority in Burma: The Rise and Decline of an Immigrant Community* (London, 1971).

R. J. COUGHLIN, *Double Identity: The Chinese in Modern Thailand* (Hong Kong, 1960).

*HAN SUYIN, *A Many-Splendoured Thing* (London, 1952) (novel).

GUY HUNTER, *South East Asia: Race, Culture and Nation* (London, 1966).

AREND LIJPHART, *The Trauma of Decolonization: The Dutch and West New Guinea* (New Haven, Conn. 1966).

VICTOR PURCELL, *The Chinese in Malaya* (London, 1948).

JOHN SLIMMING, *Malaysia: Death of a Democracy* (London, 1969).

HUGH TINKER, *The Union of Burma: A Study of the First Years of Independence*, 4th ed. (London, 1967).

AMRY AND MARY BELLE VANDENBOSCH, *Australia Faces Southeast Asia* (Lexington, Ky., 1967).

Southern Africa

T. BULL, *Rhodesia: Crisis of Colour* (Chicago, Ill., 1968).

RUTH FIRST, JONATHAN STEELE AND CHRISTABEL GURNEY, *The South African Connection: Western Investment in Apartheid* (London, 1972).

JOHN FISHER, *The Afrikaners* (London, 1969).

PETER FRAENKEL, *The Namibians of South West Africa* (London, 1974) (M.R.G.).

RICHARD GIBSON, *African Liberation Movements: Contemporary Struggles against White Minority Rule* (London, 1972).

JIM HOAGLAND, *South Africa: Civilizations in Conflict* (Boston, 1972).
* TREVOR HUDDLESTONE, *Naught for Your Comfort* (London, 1956).
DORIS LESSING, *The Grass Is Singing* (London, 1950) (novel).
——, *Martha Quest* (London, 1952) (novel).
* NELSON MANDELA, *No Easy Walk to Freedom* (London, 1965).
ALAN PATON, *Cry the Beloved Country* (London, 1948) (novel).
* MICHAEL SCOTT, *A Time To Speak* (London, 1958).
* N. SITHOLE, *African Nationalism* (Cape Town, 1962).
UNESCO, *The Effects of Apartheid on Education, Science, Culture and Information in South Africa* (Paris, 1967).
P. L. VAN DEN BERGHE, *South Africa: A Study in Conflict* (Middletown, Conn., 1965).

United States

EARL ANTHONY, *Picking up the Gun: A Report on the Black Panthers* (New York, 1970).
* JAMES BALDWIN, *Go Tell It on the Mountain* (New York, 1953) (novel).
STOKELY CARMICHAEL AND C. V. HAMILTON, *Black Power: The Politics of Liberation in America* (New York, 1971).
OLIVER C. COX, *Caste, Class and Race: A Study in Social Dynamics* (New York, 1948).
AUDRIE GIRDNER AND ANNE LOFTIS, *The Great Betrayal: The Evacuation of the Japanese-Americans during World War II* (Toronto, 1969).
MILTON GORDON, *Assimilation in America: The Role of Race, Religion and National Origin* (New York, 1964).
W. H. GRIER AND P. M. COBBS, *Black Rage* (London, 1969).
SAR A. LEVITON, W. B. JOHNSTON AND ROBERT TAGGART, *Still a Dream: The Changing Status of Blacks since 1960* (Cambridge, Mass., 1970).
* HUEY P. NEWTON, *To Die for the People* (New York, 1972).
MICHAEL NOVAK, *The Rise of the Unmeltable Ethnics: The New Political Force of the Seventies* (New York, 1971).
* BOBBY SEALE, *Seize the Time: The Story of the Black Panther Party* (London, 1970).
D. J. WEBER, *Foreigners in Their Native Land: Historical Roots of the Mexican Americans* (Albuquerque, New Mexico, 1973).
DAVID WISE AND T. B. ROSE, *The Invisible Government* [The C.I.A.] (New York, 1964).
* *The Autobiography of Malcolm X* (New York, 1965).

Western Europe

CHRISTOPHER BAGLEY, *The Dutch Plural Society: A Comparative Study in Race Relations* (London, 1973).
W. R. BÖHNING, *The Migration of Workers in the United Kingdom and Other European Countries* (London, 1972).
STEPHEN CASTLES AND GODULA KOSACK, *Immigrant Workers and Class Structure in Western Europe* (London, 1973).
HANS VAN HOUTE AND WILLY MELGERT, *Foreigners in Our Community: A New European Problem To Be Solved* (Amsterdam, 1972).
JONATHAN POWER AND ANNA HARDMAN, *Western Europe's Migrant Workers* (London, 1976) (M.R.G.)

General

JACQUES BARZUN, *Race: A Study in Superstition* (New York, 1965).
HERNAN SANTA CRUZ, *Racial Discrimination* (U.N., New York, 1971).
FRANTZ FANON, *The Wretched of the Earth* (London, 1965).
N. P. GIST AND A. P. DWORKIN (eds), *The Blending of Races: Marginality and Identity in World Perspective* (New York, 1972).
HAROLD ISAACS, *Idols of the Tribe: Group Identity and Political Change* (New York, 1975).
RAGHAVAN IYER (ed.), *The Glass Curtain between Asia and Europe* (London, 1965).
ROBIN JENKINS, *Exploitation: The World Power Structure and the Inequality of Nations* (London, 1970).
LEO KUPER, *Race, Class and Power: Ideology and Revolutionary Change in Plural Societies* (London, 1974).
JOHN REX, *Race, Colonialism and the City* (London, 1973).
RONALD SEGAL, *The Race War* (London, 1966).
HUGH TINKER, *The Banyan Tree: Overseas Emigrants from India, Pakistan, and Bangladesh* (Oxford, 1977).
P. L. VAN DEN BERGHE, *Race and Racism: A Comparative Perspective* (New York, 1967).
W. F. WERTHEIM, *East–West Parallels* (The Hague, 1964).
BEN WHITAKER, *The Fourth World: Victims of Group Oppression* (London, 1972).

Notes and References

1. RACE AND THE CONTEMPORARY WORLD

1. G. M. Macaulay, 'A Minute on Higher Education in India', dated 2 Feb 1835. In the same vein Tennyson wrote, 'Better fifty years of Europe than a cycle of Cathay' (*Locksley Hall*, 1842).

2. Arnold J. Toynbee, *A Study of History*, abridged version (London, 1947) p. 52.

3. An Australian writer of fiction, Beatrice Grimshaw, made her castaway hero explain why he would never marry a Polynesian: 'I respect my race . . . I will not throw back the course of evolution. I will have no son or daughter a hundred thousand years behind myself' – *White Savage Simon* (Sydney, 1919); quoted by Amirah Inglis, *Not a White Woman Safe: Sexual Anxiety and Politics in Port Moresby* (Canberra, 1974) p. 13.

4. J. Nehru, *An Autobiography* (repr. London, 1938) p. 500.

5. See Christopher Thorne, *The Limits of Foreign Policy: The West, the League and the Far Eastern Crisis of 1931–1933* (London, 1972; paperback ed. 1973).

6. European race relations revolutionaries are heavily indebted to C. Wright Mills and his conspiratorial, élitist conception of capitalism; their principal inspiration is Frantz Fanon and his *Wretched of the Earth*.

7. Stokely Carmichael's speech is reproduced in Tariq Ali (ed.), *New Revolutionaries* (London, 1969) p. 98.

2. IMPERIAL HIGH NOON

1. Inaugural address as Rector of Glasgow University, 16 November 1900.

2. Charles Wentworth Dilke, *Problems of Greater Britain* (London, 1890) part VI, 'Colonial Problems', ch. 2, 'Labour, Provident Societies, and the Poor'.

3. R. A. Huttenback, *Racism and Empire: White Settlers and Colored Immigrants in the British Self-Governing Colonies, 1830–1910* (Ithaca, N.Y., 1976) p. 141. Huttenback demonstrates how 'the Natal formula' was adapted by all the White Dominions.

4. The Asiatic Exclusion League published articles such as 'The Hindu: The Filth of Asia' (*The White Man*, San Francisco, Aug 1910).

5. P. C. Campbell, *Chinese Coolie Emigration* (London, 1923).

6. For a detailed description of this emigration, see Hugh Tinker, *A New System of Slavery: The Export of Indian Labour Overseas, 1830–1920* (London, 1974).

7. The Kenya episode is narrated in detail in Hugh Tinker, *Separate and Unequal: India and the Indians in the British Commonwealth, 1920–1950* (London, 1976) ch. 2, 'The Claim for Equality'.

8. Gunnar Myrdal, 'Biases in Social Research', in Arne Tiselius and Sam Nilsson (eds), *The Place of Value in a World of Facts* (Stockholm, 1970) p. 157.

9. The exposure of colonial exploitation was the work of intellectuals, not socialist party workers; see especially J. A. Hobson, *Imperialism: A Study* (London, 1902), and Paul Louis, *Le Colonialisme* (Paris, 1905).

10. Graham Wallas, *Human Nature in Politics*, 4th ed. (London, 1948) pp. 107–8.

11. The claim for equality on behalf of India forms the starting-point of Tinker, *Separate and Unequal*, which examines the subject in much greater detail.

12. Indian Legislative Assembly Debates, 7 Sep 1925.

13. *Migration within the British Commonwealth*, Cmd. 6658 (H.M.S.O., London, 1945).

14. R. A. Ferrell, *American Diplomacy: A History* (New York, 1959) p. 245.

15. Harold Nicolson, *Peacemaking 1919* (London, 1933) p. 145.

16. However, James Wilson states that 'a reasonable and moderate assessment' of pre-Conquest Amerindians would be 30 million, of whom about 2 million were in North America—see his *Canada's Indians* (Minority Rights Group, London, 1974).

3. THE MELTING-POT OF WAR

1. Alfred Zimmern, *The Third British Empire* (London, 1926) p. 84.

2. A French colonial administrator has written: 'The 175,000 soldiers enrolled during the years 1914–18 dug the grave of the old Africa in the trenches of France and Flanders', but this is viewing the situation from the viewpoint of 1950, not 1920. See Rupert Emerson, *From Empire to Nation: The Rise to Self-Assertion of Asian and African Peoples* (Cambridge, Mass., 1960) p. 24.

3. D. W. Brogan, *The Price of Revolution* (London, 1951) p. 144.

4. See H. Krausnick *et al.*, *Anatomy of the S.S. State* (New York, 1973).

5. In the 1970s Bose remains a popular hero—perhaps the most popular—for the people of India. Many refuse to believe that he died in an air-crash in 1945 and expect him to return one day. The Bose cult excludes many of his lifetime characteristics: for example, he took an Austrian wife or mistress by whom he had a daughter, but this fact is removed from the legend of the ascetic warrior.

6. Audrie Girdner and Ann Loftis, *The Great Betrayal: The Evacuation of the Japanese-Americans during World War II* (Toronto, 1969) p. 277. This is the definitive study.

7. Ibid., p. 125.

8. D. R. Hughes and Evelyn Kallen, *The Anatomy of Racism: Canadian Dimensions* (Montreal, 1974).

9. Christopher Thorne, 'Britain and the Black G.I.s: Racial Issues and Anglo-American Relations in 1942', *New Community*, Summer 1974.

10. S. Gopal, *Jawaharlal Nehru: A Biography*, vol. 1: *1889–1947* (London, 1975) p. 301.

11. Thakin Nu, *Burma under the Japanese* (London, 1954) p. 77.

12. For the story of Aung San's breakthrough to independence told in detail, see Hugh Tinker, *The Union of Burma: A Study of the First Years of Independence*, 4th ed. (London, 1967).

13. Before the British-Indian forces pulled out of Indonesia, the frugal Dutch presented a bill for rent of the barracks and port installations occupied by the British forces. Regrettably, the British declined to pay.

14. The question was posed by D. W. Brogan, 'The Illusion of American Omnipotence', *Harper's Magazine*, Dec 1952.

15. William J. Lederer and Eugene Burdick, *The Ugly American* (1958): one of the most overrated books of its time, and now almost forgotten. Presumably it was intended as a reply to Graham Greene's *The Quiet American* (London, 1955) which had exposed the harm done in Vietnam by ignorant American idealism. Greene's satire described the unconscious racism of meddling Americans, and this unconscious racism is a marked feature of *The Ugly American*. Curiously, 'the Ugly American' became a synonym for all that was worst in America's intervention, though in the book Homer Atkins (who is so described) is the hero who will defeat communism by teaching the peasants to grow more beans.

16. Diem was aware that the C.I.A. intended to do away with him, and gave international publicity to the coming event. See D. J. Duncanson, *Government and Revolution in Vietnam* (London, 1968) pp. 338–9.

4. THE END OF EMPIRE

1. W. P. Kirkman, *Unscrambling an Empire: A Critique of British Colonial Policy, 1956–1966* (London, 1966).
2. This subject is considered in detail in Tinker, *Separate and Unequal*, ch. 10, 'The Moment of Equality'.
3. Nicholas Mansergh (ed.), *Documents and Speeches on Commonwealth Affairs, 1952–1962* (London, 1963).
4. The Americans retained Okinawa, in spite of continued Okinawan protest, as a vital military base, until 1972. In that year, sustained pressure by the government of Japan (now fully rehabilitated as a bastion of private enterprise and a leading member of the Club of Ten) induced the United States to hand back this valuable piece of real estate. Thereafter, the Americans still retained a chain of bases in Okinawa, stationed 40,000 troops there, and operated the radio 'Voice of America' from there.
5. Kalman H. Silvert, *The Conflict Society: Reaction and Revolution in Latin America* (American Field Staff, rev. ed. 1966).
6. An account (which somewhat idealises Dag Hammarskjöld's role) is given by Ralph Bunche, 'The United Nations Operation in the Congo', in Andrew Cordier and Wilder Foote (eds), *The Quest for Peace* (New York, 1965).
7. Richard Gibson, *African Liberation Movements: Contemporary Struggles against White Minority Rule* (London, 1972). In retrospect, it is clear that Gibson underestimated the capacity of these movements.
8. Daniel Moynihan, the former U.S. ambassador to the United Nations who has a talent for the telling phrase, termed the Cubans 'the Gurkhas of Revolution'. (Gurkha soldiers from Nepal served the British from 1815 down to the present on battlefields throughout the world.) Moynihan alleged that Cubans were with the Syrian forces confronting Israel on the Golan Heights.
9. See Hugh Tinker, *Ballot Box and Bayonet: People and Government in Emergent Asian Countries*, 2nd ed. (London, 1966).
10. J. S. Furnivall, *Colonial Policy and Practice: A Comparative Study of Burma and Netherlands India* (Cambridge, 1948) p. 304.
11. United Nations, Population Studies no. 28, *The Future Growth of World Population* (New York, 1958) p. 24.

5. A DEFENSIVE WEST

1. Michael Novak, *The Rise of the Unmeltable Ethnics, the New Political Force of the Seventies* (New York, 1971). Harold Isaacs comments: 'As some of them now seem to see it, the [melting-]pot itself was used by the wicked Wasps of the Old North-East to boil away all the rich pure stuff of non-Waspness and cook up a great thin mess of pasty second-class Waspness which then became the essence of the common American culture' – see his *Idols of the Tribe: Group Identity and Political Change* (New York, 1975) p. 210.
2. Quoted by Louis E. Lomax, *The Negro Revolt* (New York, 1962) p. 77.
3. Milton L. Barron, 'Recent Developments in Minority and Race Relations', *The Annals* (Philadelphia, July 1975) p. 171.
4. Duane Lockwood, 'Race Policy', p. 273 in vol. VI: *Policies and Policymaking*, in F. I. Greenstein and N. W. Polsby (eds), *Handbook of Political Science* (Reading, Mass., 1975).

5. Earl Anthony, *Picking Up the Gun: A Report on the Black Panthers* (New York, 1970).

6. Dr Soyinka, an African scholar, writes: 'The study of African civilization became the sole guarantee of a fragile racial truce in American institutions all over the country. . . . Those who had the misfortune to experience the quality of the exposition . . . have had cause to be grateful when . . . the immediate crisis defused, a quiet phasing out of African studies had begun.'

7. H. Isaacs, op. cit., p. 201.

8. These West Indian immigrants joined Canada's own native blacks—a forgotten community, some of whom arrived in the 1780s with the United Empire Loyalists from the former American colonies, while others came in the 1860s via the 'underground railway' which passed fugitive slaves from the American South into Canada.

9. The police are empowered to make arrests for 'loitering with intent to commit a crime' or, in other words, on suspicion. The rate of arrests on this score is twice as high among black as among white teenagers. See also J. R. Lambert, *Crime, Police and Race Relations: A Study in Birmingham* (London, 1970).

10. A much fuller account of the immigration from South Asia is given in Hugh Tinker, *The Banyan Tree: Overseas Emigrants from India, Pakistan and Bangladesh* (Oxford, 1977).

11. Quoted in Jonathan Power and Anna Hardman, *Western Europe's Migrant Workers* (Minority Rights Group, London, 1976) p. 20.

12. Christopher Bagley, *The Dutch Plural Society: A Comparative Study in Race Relations* (London, 1973).

6. STRATEGIES OF THIRD WORLD ADVANCE

1. For a contemporary account of the Bandung conference, see George Kahin, *The Asian—African Conference* (Ithaca, N.Y., 1956). See also David Kimche, *The Afro-Asian Movement* (Jerusalem, 1973).

2. G. H. Jansen, *Afro-Asia and Non-Alignment* (London, 1966) p. 306.

3. V. Onteil, 'The Decolonization of the Writing of History', in I. Wallerstein (ed.), *Social Change: The Colonial Situation* (New York, 1966).

4. Kimche, op. cit., p. 183.

5. C. H. Malik, 'The United Nations as Ideological Battleground', in E. Berkeley Tompkins (ed.), *The United Nations in Perspective* (Stanford, Calif., 1972) p. 19.

6. See Tinker, *Separate and Unequal*, pp. 296–301.

7. Ibid., pp. 324–5.

8. For a fuller account, see Peter Fraenkel, *The Namibians of South West Africa* (Minority Rights Group, London, 1974).

9. R. W. Cox and H. K. Jacobson, *The Anatomy of Influence: Decision Making in International Organizations* (New Haven, Conn., 1973).

10. UNESCO, *The Effects of Apartheid on Education, Science, Culture and Information in South Africa* (Paris, 1967).

11. Cox and Jacobson, op. cit., p. 359.

12. An excellent summary of the record, with full references to U.N. documents, is given in A. R. Preiswerk, 'Race and Colour in International Relations', *The Year Book of World Affairs, 1970* (London, 1970).

13. Harold Isaacs, 'Color in World Affairs', *Foreign Affairs* (New York, Jan 1969) 238.

14. Leland M. Goodrich, *The United Nations in Perspective* (New York, 1959) p. 308.

15. *The Times*, 6 Nov 1963.

16. Ibid., 26 Jan 1965.

17. For a fuller account, see Colin Smith, *The Palestinians* (Minority Rights Group, London, 1975).

18. The misfortunes of the overseas Indians in South-east Asia and Africa are discussed in much greater detail in Hugh Tinker, *The Banyan Tree* (Oxford, 1977).

19. Cynthia Enloe, 'Foreign Policy and Ethnicity in "Soft" States', in Wendell Bell and W. E. Freeman (eds), *Ethnicity and Nation-Building* (Beverly Hills, Calif., 1974) p. 230.

20. Despite Castro's declaration that Cuba is an Afro-Latin country, Cuba did not demonstrate solidarity with the Africans by walking out of the Olympic Games in 1976. It was more important to demonstrate the prowess of Cuban athletes (which they did most effectively).

21. *The Times*, 10 November 1976. The conservative government of New Zealand abruptly reversed its previous clearly enunciated policy of facilitating sporting contacts with South Africa.

7. THE RACIAL SPIRAL

1. *The Civil and Military Gazette* (Lahore, 24 July and 5 Sep 1906). This was the paper on which Rudyard Kipling had been a 'cub' reporter.

2. For Mitchell's words, see Tinker, *Separate and Unequal*, p. 271. *The Oxford English Dictionary* does not include 'racialism' in its main volumes, but only in the Supplement, where the first use of the term given dates from 1907. At that time, its use was confined to the separation between English and Afrikaners in South Africa.

3. The term 'racism' is too recent to find a place in most dictionaries. However, the new extensively revised *Encyclopaedia Britannica* (1974) includes a long article under the heading 'Racism' (vol. xv).

4. Ruth First, Jonathan Steele and Christabel Gurney, *The South African Connection: Western Investment in Apartheid* (London, 1972); Colin Leys, *Underdevelopment in East Africa: The Political Economy of Neo-Colonialism, 1964–1971* (London, 1975).

Index